Class Is (always) In Session

Certain Thoughts During Uncertain Times

Daniel Francis

Alive 'n Well, LLC
PO Box 272165
Tampa, FL 33688
813-586-4856
www.alivenwell.net

ISBN: 9798750572892

DEDICATION

To Alice:
wife, teacher, coach, friend, listener, lover, soulmate,
inspiration and relentless companion. Your positivity and
goodness inspire me; your strength and wisdom keep me
alive and well!

Thank you for being a teacher as well as a classmate on
this amazing journey.

As Hammarskjold wrote,
"For all that has been, Thank you.
For all that is to come, Yes!"

ACKNOWLEDGMENTS

To the many mentors, teachers, guides and gurus of my
life: some of whom I name in this work; others will know
from my writing that they are the source of my gleanings.

Preface

Two months after the COVID-19 became "real" in the United States, my wife and created a website, www.alivenwell.net. Why? The confluence of the negativity surrounding politics, the pandemic and racial tensions compelled us, as we say in our mission statement, to promote a positive "virus" in the world.

While many people find it difficult--if not impossible--to keep focused on the good and beautiful, our work through the website (webinars, daily quotes and blogs) is to embrace and remind others of truths such as these:

- To live a less frantic life
- To let things unfold in their time
- To embrace this moment now and giving it our full attention
- To have relentless pragmatism and unbridled persistence
- To possess indefatigable ingenuity
- To get unstuck and unleashed
- To turn negative situations into positive opportunities

These are certainly our greatest gifts to ourselves and to one another!

What you are reading is an edited compilation of the 15 months of blog reflections I have written on our website as well as transcripts from our podcast, "At the Well."

It is my sincere hope that these reflections will inspire those who are awake to become more healthy and those who are well to grow to be more grateful and aware.

Daniel Francis

Keep Your Distance- But Only Physically

Something seemed amiss.

We quickly understood what was meant by the directive "social distancing." We know it's to help slow the infection and flatten the curve.

But please do not take it *literally*.

It never meant to keep us away socially, only bodily.

Few things can be more important at times like these than reaching out by phone, text, email or Zoom.

As neighbors, it's ironic that to show how much we care is to dodge one another on the sidewalk- but only physically, never personally.

A "Hello" or "How are you?" and "Stay healthy" will keep us close and in this together, no matter the skin tone.

Something we miss- hugs and handshakes, kisses and caresses- can, for now, be replaced by more social closeness, even if it's 6 feet away.

Monday Mornings

I don't know how young I was when I heard The Carpenters croon out "Rainy Days and Mondays Always Bring Me Down." I have read of studies that seem to indicate that people who live in cloudy and rainy places on earth have a higher incidence of depression-- or worse.

I'm grateful to my sister, Felicia, who coached me once on a family vacation back in the early 2000s. We seven siblings and spouses and children and my father were at a beach house and the last two days were overcast, even threatening rain. My sister's response: "Never let the weather outside affect the weather inside."

So, if Monday as a day of the week has some crazy control over your heart or soul (or body), don't let it.

Ask yourself: what surprise...what amazing thing... will I learn or read or hear or smell or eat today?

Daniel Francis

Presence

When I was working in NYC, I would pass a corner diner
called "Eat Here Now." I thought it funny and impressive
that in three words the establishment was telling a
prospective customer a) What to do; b) Where to do it;
and c) When to do it.

Eckhart Tolle reminds us that "When you make the
present moment, instead of past and future, the focal point
of your life, your ability to enjoy what you do and with it
the quality of your life increases dramatically."

What if we could live here now? I don't mean without
making necessary plans, or budgeting or editing that
Amazon Subscribe and Save. Imagine if we could let the
moments of this day pass thru--almost one by one--being
aware of them and not judging them and thinking the next
one might be better.

Too Many, Too Few

This past week, my wife's aunt died. Besides being an amazing woman, she was also the last of Alice's uncles and aunts to pass away- at 99 ½ years of age!

My mom died when she was only 70. I was 31 at the time and--even then—her death seemed too young, too premature.

Part of what I know is that there are people who are <u>alive</u>-- meaning they breath, eat, mow the lawn, watch tv-- and yet they are not well. Perhaps there is something in their past, in their craw, in their heart that goes on poisoning them. Or there is a sickness in their body that feels as if it chokes them if they get "too far."

Then there are those who are <u>well</u>-- physically fit, active gym-goers or daily exercisers or at least they take vitamins and supplements and avoid red meat or embrace paleo or keto diets... but they are not alive. They move through life at times on autopilot and seem to be overly sensitive or insensitive... it doesn't matter. Truth is, they just are not awake.

That's precisely why my wife and I have began <u>www.alivenwell.net</u>. We want to share with whoever cares to listen what we know that works: a life of balance, joy, peace and gratitude never fails to amaze us and inspire deep delight.

For this, we are forever thankful for the examples of our parents and wonderful aunts such as +Lola and my last living aunt, Zia Madelba!

Daniel Francis

Bigger Love

Last night we watched a beautiful and humorous Father's Day TV special hosted by pop artist John Legend. Besides showing us into his home and dazzling us with the beauty of his two children, he featured his wife, friends (by phone, of course- we're still physically distancing) and a few of his songs.

A new song he wrote is entitled "Bigger Love" and some lyrics are as follows:

> The world feels like it's crumbling
> Everyday, another new something
> But in the end, in the end
> Can't nobody do us in

I'm not sure if Legend is addressing the world in which we live now (with a contagion, protests and economic strain), but here is a song-writer telling us the truth that in the end, it's "all about loving."

That's loving big! That's *legend*ary love.

Waiting And Wading

As a new (7-year) transplant to Florida, there is still so much to learn about the Sunshine State. Although we are made fun of all too often (sometimes deservingly), the rich history, diverse cultures, natural beauty and excellent weather are some of the reasons why 1,000 people move here every day.

My wife introduced me to the amazing natural photography of long-time Floridian Clyde Butcher. Recently, he wrote about adjusting to disability after a stroke as well as the challenges of living the life of quarantine. He is making the most of this time and finds life and nature to be good.

Clyde Butcher writes:

> We recently spent a week exploring Highlands Hammock, the oldest State Park in Florida.
>
> The peace, quiet and sounds of birds singing to each other has relaxed us, as nature always does.
>
> I waited an hour and a half for clouds to cover the sun in order to get even light for the photograph I was taking. The act of waiting was a form of meditation...watching the ripples running through the reflection of the trees in the water, the sounds of birds, the small breeze that make the trees dance...all of it was just what we needed...what we all need.

Daniel Francis

Born On The 4th Of July

From the toddler who doesn't want to hold Mommy's hand (for a moment) to the child who can ride a bike without training wheels to the teenager who leaves home for college or a career, there's something about independence that has its own origin and power. That I-can-do-it-myself spirit is both a sign of natural growth as well as healthy individuation.

When "these" United States of America decided that taxation without representation was not helping our young republic form itself, the training wheels came off and an amazing experiment in democracy was born.

And yet... we still are growing and maturing. As a nation, the teenage "acne" of racial discrimination persists, and we've still got some work to do about that glass ceiling and equal gender pay.

The good news is that, except for the violence of peripheral protesting, our country can handle this continuing revolution. The word itself can mean circling and rolling.

Perhaps this is the liminal dance that freedom requires; and the correctives, while scary for some, are contractions that signal a new birthing.

As the character who plays the hotel proprietor in the movie *The Best Exotic Marigold Hotel* says: "The only real failure is the failure to try, and the measure of success is how we cope with disappointment."

Search And Replace

Unlike my brothers who are self-taught carpenters since
their teens, I'm new to home improvements (after having
spent 20 years in church rectories). I'm okay with basic
electrical and plumbing, but forget about spackling a hole
in the wall- just ask my wife. A few months ago, we
decided that rather than trying to repair a hole, we'd cover
it up. So we found and purchased a sign that says
"Thankful. Grateful. Blessed."

For many, Thanksgiving is a top favorite holiday. What's
not to love about the mirthful mingling of family, friends,
food, football and traditions? No wonder some folks look
forward to it all year and has become unofficially the start
of the Christmas season- trees and decorations get put up
and a fire made even if it's 70 degrees outside!

And yet, it's different this year.

The pandemic has been brutal on everyone and now it's
disrupting our Thanksgiving.

But someone online recently shared that each of her Zoom
recovery meetings starts with a passage called "Just for
Today." Here's a snippet:

> Just for today, my thoughts will be on those who
> love me
>
> Just for today, my thoughts are on my blessings
>
> Just for today, my thoughts are on one thing I'm
> grateful for

Isn't it true that an attitude of appreciation does wonders
for replacing what's wrong with what's right....that looking
on the bright side is not just a nice idea but rather an
energizing intention?

Daniel Francis

There are cracks and holes and imperfections galore in our lives, country and world right now.

Actually, they've always been there. What's happened is that they are more noticeable (and perhaps more aggravating) during these havoc-wreaking times.

Maybe signs only cover holes in the wall, but they point to something else: we have tremendous power in the decision to see things differently through a more positive lens. For that, this Thanksgiving and always, let us be "thankful and grateful" for we are surely "blessed!"

Beyond The Pandemic

My wife's parents were only one years old when the 1918
flu struck

I read in high school about the Great Depression of 1929-
1933

My parents didn't talk about it much but they worked hard

My father was in World War II and lost a few good
buddies

A cousin went to Korea, and I watched Vietnam on TV

I was living in NYC when the towers fell in 2001

And who can forget anthrax in the mail?

You can add many other events personal and global that
have made us pause, even cry.

And yet... what I know is that somehow, in some way and
in some time we will be able to pull ourselves together and
get through this.

I like the saying from Victoria, Australia: "Staying Apart
Keeps Us Together"

We have scars to show- there is no doubt.

Horror stories abound but also heroic accounts and
amazing triumphs from essential workers to parents
working, then returning home to cook, clean, bathe and
read a story.

As someone I know said weeks before he died of cancer,
"We can handle this. We can handle this."

Time is not ticking like a bomb or as "sands through an
hourglass."

This is truly a Phoenix moment, a metamorphosis:

We can get through this. We will get through it!

You Are Quite... Becoming

Our website generates a "Daily Dose"—the quotes we send out daily—and every now and then I come upon a maxim that speaks volumes by itself and yet invites application for today.

For instance, recently I read this quote from Henry David Thoreau: "What you get by achieving your goals is not as important as what you become by achieving your goals."

It makes me think of how often people make resolutions (at New Year's, when turning 30 or 60, etc.) and what happens when the goal is thwarted by some distraction, weakness or "second thought."

What's vital is to remember that the process of goal-setting can be truly liberating. You are in a real sense seeing beyond what you are now into a future that looks and feels better- otherwise, you wouldn't be setting the goal in the first place. You are... becoming.

In evolutionary terms, we've graduated from lizard brains to the limbic system to the amazing 3 lbs. that we have now between our temples.

Trouble is, the lizard brain doesn't know what delayed gratification is and the limbic system is all about emotions and memory. But when you place a good higher than other things, your "stretching" for that goal becomes you.

In a nutshell, this is what coaching is about: holding up the best of you reminding you it is true and real and then assisting you in formulating concrete steps to reach your goals.

Munching On Memories

On the exact day of the month we got married and for every month of that first year, no matter the weather or temperature, my wife and I had a ritual: go to the grocery store to pick up a pre-ordered cake (identical to the one we had for our wedding) then head to the Gulf of Mexico, about 50 minutes from our home. Twice we got there only to take a quick walk before sunset (due to the job I had at the time); another month it was so cold (yes, in Tampa!) that we ate our cake in the car; but it never rained and on many occasions we were able to swim and sun and read and eat, enjoying the mostly isolated beach time.

Due to COVID-19 we're trying to do our part to flatten the curve and so we've not been to the beach and probably won't for the remainder of the year. We're fine with that- it's a small price to pay for the overall health of our city, state, country and world. The wonderful thing is that we hold memories of our twelve months of beach trips and have the confidence that we'll return- shortly, we hope.

Perhaps the wisdom during this time is what we saw once on a sign: Seek Out Calm Waters. Yes, you can boogie board or surf the waves or float on your back or sit and splash...but there is that place just beyond the breaking waves that is an oasis. Sometimes it's even a sandbar you can stand on.

Like this pandemic, the onus (and opportunity) for us is to look for and find new places of peace- harbors in the storm, jetties for protection.

Maybe for you that's a meditation app or a walk in a park, maintaining physical distancing. Maybe you can try yoga for the first time or take it up again after many years, or click on a YouTube stretching video that connects you with your body and links you to your inner fulcrum.

Daniel Francis

You see, our primal posture is peace. What the beach (or your favorite place) does is simply REMIND us of what is inside.

Find your own oasis.

Seek out your calm seas amidst these crazy times.

Your future self with thank you and it will provide memorable munchies for grateful grazing.

Chooseday (aka Tuesday)

I know.

It's a corny title.

Anyone who knows me understands that I like to play with words....and, okay, am a bit corny.

So it's Tuesday and yet every day is "chooseday"- meaning, we have the choice how we are going to frame this day.

To be clear: we don't choose much of what comes our way, but we can guide how we receive and handle it. That's the "framing" part of our choice-making today and everyday.

For example, why is it that some people don't get upset with other drivers or insulting Facebook posts or that the store is still out of Clorox wipes? Is it because they were endowed with more patience or that they don't care?

No, you see these folks have learned the life lesson of knowing what things can be controlled and what can't.

Think about it: why would you ever want to cede your power and--more importantly, your peace-- over to someone else?

And yet, isn't that what happens when we get upset by what someone else has done or said or didn't do or say?

Let today be your chooseday: YOU be the one to select your emotions and actions (and reactions). Resist letting someone else steal what ultimately is your unalienable right to freedom. You do not need to have your emotions hijacked by someone else's dangerous driving or temperamental tweets.

Daniel Francis

As spiritual writer Eknath Easwaran writes:

> As human beings, we have been born with the
> capacity to make choices. No other creature has
> this capacity, and no human being can avoid this
> responsibility. Every day, whether we see it or not,
> we have a choice of two alternatives in what we
> do, say, and think. These alternatives are: what is
> pleasant and what is beneficial. The first pleases us
> now. The second may be unpleasant at the
> beginning, as anyone who has begun a physical
> fitness program knows; but it will improve our
> health and contribute to our peace of mind. Both
> choices promise satisfaction. One we get
> immediately, but it comes and goes; the other
> requires effort, but its benefits stay with us and
> often benefit those around us as well.

Have a good chooseday!

What Are You Missing?

I've read that sometimes a person who's had a leg amputated feels a phantom itch and might even reach to scratch non-existent skin. I wonder if the body is missing a part of itself and tricks the mind as a way of re-membering.

Some of our friends are doing well, adapting to these strange times. Others are experiencing "cabin fever" or even low-grade depression. I can understand that. My wife and I miss eating at our local haunts and supporting independent businesses. We don't go to the cinema often but do miss that opportunity. We are adapting to going without some things. Truthfully, most of what we go without is not essential.

But it seems that there are indefinable, wordless aches that are creating a sense of loss in many people. Our friend Keen pointed us to a podcast called *On Being* with Krista Tippett- specifically, an episode called "Navigating Loss Without Closure." Tippet's guest, Pauline Boss, came up with the term "ambiguous loss."

I remember back in 2001 when my mom died at age 70. She, my father and a lot of the family were at the First Communion of my twin nieces when suddenly she collapsed and died of a heart attack. I certainly mourned her death, as did many others.

But even years later there was something beyond words that would taint family celebrations and life events. How glad I was that some of my siblings were there for that dinner the night before she died and witnessed the secular *viaticum* the day of her passing; but my not having closure-- not being able to say "good-bye"--lingered in me for many years.

17

Daniel Francis

I felt the presence of her absence, as if part of me had
been amputated.

Is this lockdown/stay-at-home/safer-at-home/mask-
wearing/hand-washing/6-feet-distancing/new abnormal
taking its toll on you? Then be gentle with yourself.
Sometimes it's the indescribable hurt or loss that can sneak
up on you. If it eventually breaks open your heart- good.
If it breaks your spirit, give me a call. No, seriously.
That's what I do!

A Comet of Errors

Alice recently posted this quote from Martin Luther King, Jr for her Daily Dose: "Only in the darkness can you see the stars."

But it didn't work!

I should clarify. We waited for the darkness and were able to see the planets Jupiter, Saturn and Mars (maybe even Neptune), but our attempts at seeing the recently discovered comet, Neowise, were unsuccessful. As directed by a reliable website, we waited 1 1/2 hours after sunset and drove to an empty parking lot. Through our binoculars, we had a few false sightings. Then the mosquitoes had true sightings and tastings of me. To move away from them, I accidentally walked into a mound of fire ants and still have the bumps to show. Then without warning the sprinklers came on and doused me. Okay, it was time to move on from there.

Back in our neighborhood, there were too many trees to get a confirmable sighting, despite a handy iPhone app. We tried over the next several evenings, but clouds obscured the night sky.

Sometimes, merely desire and good intention are not enough.

In the 1300s, a German Dominican named Heinrich Suso wrote:

> In the first days of my youth I tried to find it in the creatures, as I saw others do; but the more I sought, the less I found it, and the nearer I went to it, the further off it was. For of every image that appeared to me, before I had fully tested it, or abandoned myself to peace in it, an inner voice

said to me: "This is not what thou seekest."

Back to 2020, despite the bites and bother, perhaps the searching is enough, just as they say the journey-ing is the destination. No one alive now will have the chance to see Neowise again- it will not be visible for another 7,000 years. But just knowing that this celestial visitor skirted our planet and that a lot of people saw it is itself a wonder and a gift.

It would have been fun and satisfying to have seen it ourselves, but we joy in continuing to seek.

Beyond Boundaries

What I know is that many times I limit myself mentally because I've confined my thinking to a narrow perspective.

For example, many of you might be familiar with the (true?) story of the truck that got stuck at the entrance of one of NYC's tunnels. It was too tall and it jammed in fairly well. Reversing the engine was not working. Workers were about to call in big equipment when some boy--who had gotten out of the car since traffic had stopped--suggested letting air out of the tires. It worked and I'm sure some grown-ups' egos were deflated like innertubes.

In some self-help programs, Einstein's definition of insanity is quoted: "To do the same thing over and over expecting different results."

What is it today...this week that you might look at differently? Maybe it's a person you might regard differently (with more patience, understanding or compassion)?

Imagine this: seeing something from a different vantage can change the way we view it! Who doesn't want that? Then boundaries become smaller and options more abundant.

Daniel Francis

Unfolding

It's been five months since the first United States fatality due to COVID-19. No matter where you are on the spectrum of opinions regarding policy, protection and prevention, few can argue that the pandemic has changed our lives and ended many others. On our daily walk around the neighborhood, we've noticed that a woman has a sign in her yard which she changes every now and then. One day it read: "Do What Is Yours To Do." I find that to be maddeningly simple and yet eminently practical.

This pandemic is one of the reasons why we began www.alivenwell.net, and a major reason why we named it "Alive 'n Well". What is ours to do is to provide an increasingly wide variety of possibilities for you and (with your help) the people you love.

So what is yours to do? Isn't it such a simple yet complicated question? It's simple because we all can do something: be kind(er), less reactive, more proactive, have a deeper awareness of our connection to the world, etc.

But it's also complicated because we can become beset by doubt about our own perceived puny effort or scattered energy. May I suggest that it's not only the consequence of our good actions but rather what the actions do to us internally. We begin unfolding doggy-eared pages that we promised we'd return to years ago.

Remember?

Among Us

These wet summer days provide our yard with much-needed rain. Great for our plants and grass, this moisture can also be a catalyst for fungus, particularly mushrooms. Also known as toadstools, they are curiously fast growers. Seemingly overnight, their umbrella tops stretch out supported by ribbed gills. Alice enjoys the edible kind; I'd rather eat pencil-tip erasers.

Fungi get their nutrition from metabolizing non-living organic matter- meaning, they break down and "eat" dead plants just as a compost pile does. Isn't it amazing- the opportunism of nature? Nothing is wasted.

As a child growing up in Maryland, I had my summer belly full of crabs, only later to understand they are bottom feeders. Vultures (and eagles, when not fishing) are notorious for feasting on roadkill. And how many a college student, after too many late-night coffees, discovered penicillin in unwashed mugs.

So don't be surprised at what is growing in and around you these days. Perhaps you've cultivated a new skill or become more appreciative of old talents. Maybe the detritus of this disease will have become fodder for deeper concerns and higher values.

I hope so.

Let's take this opportunity of staying at home by becoming more at home with ourselves. When you think about it, is there really a better personal outcome?

Daniel Francis

Sifting And Settling

I worked in Alaska for three summers in a town called
North Pole. In the area there were old mines that
attracted tourists for "sure thing" gold panning. You bring
up sand and clay and, if you're lucky, find a gold flake or
two (it is suggested to use tweezers to pick up your
findings). I never did it, but a couple of summers ago
here in Florida I was excited to find my first shark's tooth.
No sifting needed- it was right there on the beach as we
were doing the Sanibel Stoop.

Every three months, my Google Calendar reminds me to
change our home's AC filter. I'm always amazed at how
much dust it traps (and whatever else is floating in the air).
When we have our routine HVAC maintenance we are
told that a regularly changed filter will save us a lot of
money by eliminating preventable repairs down the road.

I wonder how much "stuff" is in the air that I mindlessly
take in, forgetting to sift and filter. There's so much in the
news that is really not new, but old, re-heated
polarizations. Rather than fueling the fire of disagreement
(and the consequent siloing of groups and positions), what
if we choose to listen respectfully and hear, truly HEAR,
the pain or worry or values or fears coming from someone
with whom we don't agree?

What does it cost us to hold our tongue (and opinion)
sometimes and watch with loving concern and authentic
interest?

There's a celebrated story about a disciple who asks his
teacher's counsel to avoid overacting and impulsivity. The
teacher hands him a pitcher and invites the student to fill it
up from the nearby pond and then to observe the water.
As the mud and dirt begin to fall, the teacher points out
how clear the top of the liquid is: "Thus you too can learn

to let your emotions and opinions settle before speaking."

As A.A. Milne writes, "If the person you are talking to doesn't appear to be listening, be patient. It may simply be that he has a small piece of fluff in his ear."

Daniel Francis

T1 2 K1

Were you able to decipher the subject of this title- "T1 2 K1"? In the cyberworld of texting and a new digital shorthand, the lexicon for abbreviations and acronyms is ever-expanding. Most people have used OK as "okay" long before cell phones and iPads, but now LOL ("laughing out loud"), TY ("thank you") and IMHO ("in my humble opinion") are the "See Spot Run" of internet linguistics.

Takes One To Know One (T1 2 K1) is the subject heading. I learned it, in long-form, from a gentle and self-effacing friend several decades ago. If I complimented him on something, he would respond, "Hey, it takes one to know one!"

All of which brings me to a parable that goes something like this:

> One day as the Buddha was sitting under a tree, a slender young soldier walked by, looked at the Buddha's large belly, and remarked: "You look like a pig!"
>
> The Buddha looked up calmly at the soldier and replied: "You look like God."
>
> Taken aback by the comment, the soldier asked the Buddha: "Why do you say that I look like God?"
>
> The Buddha answered: "We don't really see what's outside of ourselves; we see what's inside of us and project it out. As I sit here I think about God so that when I look out, that's what I see. And you... you must be thinking about other things."

26

I learned years ago that generally "how you see is what you see." That's why five people can witness the same event, seemingly observe the same thing and yet each have very different versions of what happened.

This is much more than just seeing the glass half empty or half full. It's summoning within the very best of who we are and envisioning that outside of ourselves.

Daniel Francis

A Time To...

At funerals and some other occasions, the beautiful words from Ecclesiastes Chapter 3 are often read. Made singable by the Byrds during the 60s, the cadence of each juxtapositional line could serve as a lesson by itself.

Sadly, this novel virus has nonfictional statistics which make us realize that it truly is a "time to die" for some and a "time to heal" for all.

What time is it for you?

Most of us have heard the saying: "It's the journey and not the destination", but what if it's true?

Imagine if this time "in-between" is not just for waiting. Would if it will mark our memories as a different "BC & AD" (Before Covid and After Disease)? What if it became a time of learning, living thoughtfully and maybe even

A TIME OF GROWTH

- a time to slow down and learn how to Zoom our grandchildren
- a time to get back on that diet and learn to YouTube exercise routines a time to turn off the TV once in a while and learn from Ted talks
- a time to ponder some deep(er) questions and learn from The Great Courses
- a time to move beyond "what I'm missing" to "how I'm growing!"

If this--for now--is the journey, then Enjoy the Ride!

The Year That Is

For some, the year can't be over soon enough. It's as if turning the calendar to 2021 has some magical ability to wipe away the raw craziness of this year. Donald Hall warns us that "there is never a later, but for most of my life I have believed in later."

No, before we think about pressing DELETE on this year, a sieve would be helpful to keep what is beneficial and let go of the destructive.

This reminds me of a quote I first read 28 years ago:

Oh, the comfort—
the inexpressible comfort of feeling
safe with a person,
Having neither to weigh thoughts,
nor measure words—but pouring them
all right out—just as they are—
chaff and grain together—
certain that a faithful hand will
take and sift them—
keep what is worth keeping—
and with the breath of kindness
blow the rest away.

-Dinah Maria (Mulock) Craik (1826-1887)

The final line is the key: "blow the rest away." Perceive the gentle firmness of this action and you will capture the genius of the sieve.

There is no forcing but rather an organic letting go, a falling through, a separating out.

Daniel Francis

In Harmony's Way

"Your eyes are too big for your stomach."

Although she didn't coin it, my mom was the first one I
heard this phrase from. We were at the local 7-Eleven.
This didn't happen often. With seven kids and a
mortgage, snacks or meals outside of the house were a rare
treat. I saw my older brother order a Slurpee and wanted
the same thing, same size. Her warning only emboldened
me to want it more.

Of course I didn't finish it... well, not right away.
Truthfully, by the time the brain freeze was over, so was
my taste for the drink which had become a slurry mess of
liquid sugar.

Likewise, I wonder sometimes if our hearts are too small
for our souls. We want--oh how much we want-- but
settle for what rarely satisfies. The junk food of talking
heads might temporarily appetize; tweets or posts that
merely confirm my "position" might initially appease;
pointing out what's wrong with this or that might-for a
moment-appeal...but there arises a time when the deepest
part of me just craves something better, higher or deeper; I
need something more authentic, long-lasting and solid.

Maybe it might help during these times to see the bigger
picture. For example, if you were only to see a dentist
with a needle, it would look barbaric unless you know it's
Novocain and it's going to help your child with her
impacted tooth.

When I was given my Shingles shot, my body felt like I
had done a 4-hour workout! But I know what it will
prevent, and that makes all the difference. Being able to
have a wider view enables us to filter out and filter in.

30

Who doesn't want that lightness of being? It makes it so much easier to travel when you have less encumbrance. I firmly believe that by spending time in the quiet and still places within we can tap the inner, natural harmony we are designed for. To do this we need to learn how to tune out the mindless chatter that takes up vital space in our mind and heart. To be in harmony's way is like stopping your ears when a beautiful concert is playing.

As T. S. Eliot writes in *The Four Quartets:*

> "We must be still and still moving / Into another intensity / For a further union."

Daniel Francis

"...Like I Died And Went To Heaven"

My late father was in many ways a beautifully simple man.
Despite becoming Master Chief in the Navy while working
as a cryptologist in amazing places like Turkey, Morocco
and southern Spain, he kept his life uncomplicated- loved
his wife and seven kids, embraced a strong faith and did
not shirk domestic chores.

While my mom helped enormously to make ends meet by
working full-time as a floral designer, Dad got us up in the
morning for school with breakfast ready, made our bag
lunches and then went off to Ft. Meade (NSA), MD
Monday to Friday, from 8am to 6pm. When he came
home, no matter what Mom had on the stove or in the
oven, he would often say, as he greeted her with a kiss,
"Smells great! I can't wait to eat."

As much as Mom was an introverted Slovak-American,
Dad was the extroverted Italian-American. He would
make friends with anyone. Toward the end of his life,
when Alzheimer's took much of his mind away, he would
continue to display affection such as kissing the hand of
the driver who took care to seatbelt him on the bus before
taking him to what we affectionately called "Daddy Day
Care."

In his later years, when eating something he enjoyed or
spotting something amazing or hearing a song in church,
he would say, "I feel like I've died and gone to heaven."

I remember an elderly couple whom I met years ago. They
loved each other so much and had such a soulful
relationship that they told me going to heaven could only
be a "lateral move" as they were experiencing it here on
earth.

Which reminds me of one of my favorite songs by Andrea

Bocelli, called "I Believe." In it are words that inspire me, akin to my father's simplicity, to help make heaven on earth.

One day I'll hear
The laugh of children
In a world where war has been banned.
One day I'll see
Men of all colors
Sharing words of love and devotion.
Stand up and feel The Holy Spirit
Find the power of your faith.
Open your heart
To those who need you
In the name of love and devotion.
Yes, I believe.
I believe in the people
Of all nations
To join and to care for love.
I believe in a world
Where light will guide us
And giving our love
We'll make heaven on earth.
I believe.

Daniel Francis

Coherence

Not too long ago, one of my daily emails included a link to a beautiful, soothing, peace-evoking song sung virtually by 17,572 singers from 129 countries performing Eric Whitacre's "Sing Gently". One comment about this song and its production struck me as true and hopeful:

> In quantum physics, there is such a thing as coherence. Coherence is when a group of drummers is playing in rhythm at the same time. If one was out of tune, it wouldn't sound nice. You are in fact a body of energy. Either living as a coherent being, in tune. Or incoherently, out of tune and rhythm. You can move into rhythm by opening your focus to the space around you and moving into a state of love. Just like these singers, singing from their hearts. And them all coming together as one to make a beautiful symphony. Imagine if all lived with love in their hearts at the same time. What World would we live in? What World would you live in? Live in love.
>
> (posted by George Firth)

It's not difficult to recognize the incoherence in life-inconsistencies in loved ones, inaccuracies in the news, impatience in ourselves, inappropriate behavior in leaders, inertia in our flagging efforts, injustices, inequalities, indignities... you get the idea.

Might I suggest that this is when we need most to be reminded of the best that it's in us and hear the harmony and mellifluous coherence of our joint humanity.

One Person's Trash...

I subscribe to *Instructables*, an open-source website that features projects made from scratch or with ordinary objects lying around. It never fails to amaze me how creative and productive people can be when they see something differently than the rest of us.

My uncle Bob was such a one. Ever resourceful, he could fix motors and machines. On weekends, he descended upon yard sales to haggle and buy "broken" things only to repair and sell them for a handsome profit.

My wife and I also marvel at how imaginative designers get on home improvement shows. One of our favorite TV couples is Ben and Erin Napier from "Home Town". It's not uncommon for them to reclaim wood pulled from a demolished wall and convert it into a window box garden or porch swing.

Back to Instructables... one of their bylines is "A Happy Place" and reads:

> Making things makes people happy.
> We can't prove it, but we know it to be true.
> Find your happy place...

Where's your happy place? I don't mean an address or location... rather, what do you do or love that promotes your inner joy?

May I suggest that if it's not coming from within, it probably won't last long.

Perhaps some of the trash of these trying times might inspire you to consider a hidden treasure that was there all along.

Daniel Francis

Back to School

When my oldest brother became a grandfather, I felt
proud of him...and then I felt oldish. If he's a grandpop,
I'm a great uncle! His grandson is now 8 1/2 years old and
the other day I received a text-picture of him and his baby
sister ready for their first day back to school; somehow I
could pick up that new clothes smell through my phone.

Do you remember the jitters or joy (or combination of
both) the week before, the night before, your first day back
to school? I was with another brother at his house when
several of his kids were waiting for the bus at the bottom
of the hill. It was another first day back to school and
parents had set up tables of bagels and juice, fruit and
snacks.

What a wonderful way for families to celebrate this minor
rite of passage.

It seems that the longer I live the more I'm discovering
new classrooms. It is said that when the student is ready,
the teacher arrives. I'm not so sure, because there are
times when a lesson has been thrust upon me uninvited or
the test is not an open book; some answers are not
erasable and others have no grading curve mercy.

On the other side of the teacher's desk, I recall the
summer of 1986 when I was tutoring adults in poor, rural
Appalachia. What pride in their eyes when these coal
miners could finally pen their name and differentiate "V as
in valley" from "W as in water." Somehow they got
convinced that it was never too late to go back to school.
I was honored to help them get there.

The truth is that we stop learning and growing and
widening our horizon only at our peril.

A Turkish proverb suggests that one should "fear an ignorant man more than a lion." Perhaps we can all take a page from the eager kids on-line at home or masked in a classroom: to be amazed by the lessons which abound all around is to know it's not too late.

Daniel Francis

September Grass

My wife and I love doing our weekly lawn mowing, edging, weed-whacking, clipping, trimming, power blowing and yard waste-binning. Whenever we do our yardwork, we don our protective eyewear and sun hats and work boots. In our yard is an oak tree and in late summer you can see the sun dazzling the Spanish moss like laundry draped upon its limbs?

Each September I like to do yardwork with James Taylor in my ear, specifically his song called "September Grass." The first stanza evokes a feeling of change in the air and then the song harkens back to the sweetness of summers past.

Well, the sun's not so hot in the sky today
and you know I can see summertime slipping on away.
A few more geese are gone,
a few more leaves turning red,
but the grass is as soft as a feather in a featherbed.

Beautiful words, no?

How do artists do it- generating songs, scripts, sketches, stories and so many other creative expressions... and then do it again and again?

They notice.

They pay attention.

They take the time to see/hear/write what others can't or won't or are too distracted to observe.

In short, they are MINDFUL.

If you feel that the concept of mindfulness is appealing to you, or you desire to deepen what you know of it or practice, you're in luck.

As James Taylor writes, "Oh, September grass is the sweetest kind, it goes down easy like apple wine. Hope you don't mind if I pour you some, made that much sweeter by the winter to come."

May the end of your summer be sweet and may those who know you be inspired by the artful expression of your life.

Daniel Francis

Think of Laura

Although I am a huge fan of songwriter and singer
Christopher Cross (ever since the late 70s), this title
references the recent Hurricane Laura, not his song.

As I write this, the category 4 storm has just hit the
western Louisiana coast. Damage assessment and reports
will be coming in. Our hope is that most people heeded
the warnings and evacuated or made precautions.

Living in Florida, we see signs for hurricane preparedness
all the time, especially just before the "season" begins in
June. Companies that sell and install windows tout
hurricane-proof rating strength; tree companies will trim
"widow-makers" for a fee. One mayor says that she
consistently warns her people to be ready in an hour to
leave home- bags packed with important documents,
water, medicine and food for Fido.

When I was young, the code words issued by mom or dad
that "company was coming" meant to get the home ready:
empty the overflowing kitchen trash bin, clean the
bathroom, vacuum the foyer and gussy up a bit.

Years later I wonder why it took visitors to force us to
make the house nicer.

The body and psyche cannot live in a "what if" mode all
the time- the stress would eventually take its toll and
possibly lead to worse problems later on.

And yet, there's something about the 20/20 vision of
hindsight that seems to get lost on us.

I wonder if we sometimes redact yesterday's memories in
order to avoid making the changes necessary for quality
living today.

Class Is (always) In Session

What might you be postponing that, although difficult to do now, would bring you more joy once its taken care of?

Daniel Francis

The "End" of Summer

For a good two decades, I was flying as often as three times a month. In the terminal, I would see couples kiss and families embrace. It was hard to tell whether this affection marked arrivals or departures, if these were warm welcomes or four-tissue farewells.

This time of year is like that. For some, Labor Day is the unofficial close of summertime and there's a relief that cooler weather is coming; for others, it's a nameless sorrow that seems to come from a desire to hold on.

Wherever you fall on the summer spectrum, our hope is that you have had some chance to "vacate." Odd word, isn't it? But as you can probably guess, it comes from the sense of being empty, free to be filled.

I'm so grateful that despite the pandemic a private Preserve has not closed its gates. Nearly 9,000 acres of wetlands, oak hammocks, cypress domes and pine flatwoods, it's a return to the "real Florida" where you can see an alligator and an eagle, an armadillo and a stork on the same day.

Maybe the summer you had was reading a great book or (re)painting a room or returning to a craft or hobby that has beckoned for a while. Perhaps you've taken time just to be still and appreciate what is yours and yours to do. Our hope is that you have tried from time to time to be empty from your labor.

For me, there are still 14 more days until Autumn and I will be enjoying the remainder of my summer. Maybe this is why spring, summer, winter and fall are called *seasons*- they spice up our lives.

Why [not] Me?

In a podcast I heard yesterday, a professional sportsman told a familiar story: early success, lots of money, a big house, supportive wife and two kids.

Then the story went to a place familiar only to some readers- he revealed that he had cancer. When the doctor informed him of this fact, his response was not "Why me?" but rather "Why *not* me?" As a life coach, I wonder how this person was able to be ready for this news, this new normal, this "sentence."

By naming our website and initiative "Alive 'n Well", we know that many people are quite the opposite: ailing and suffering...and we know there are those who are sick and tired of being sick and tired! This is precisely why we felt compelled to begin something so positive-sounding and health-promoting.

We are also aware that there are people who are doing "okay" but could be consciously or unconsciously contributing to--or absorbing--the negativity that is rife during these strange times.

We want to do our part and lessen the impact of this kind of negativity. What about you?

Daniel Francis

The Story Goes On

On Sunday mornings, as Mom was readying the gaggle of us for Church, there was on occasion a discordance. If we were ahead of schedule (rarely for the nine of us in the Francis Family) and hair was disheveled or shirts untucked, she would admonish us to "look presentable for Mass."

But if we were running late (which was normal even if it was the last Church service), Mom would say "Let's go! God doesn't mind how you look."

Years later I know that there are very few absolutes in life, that things change and people do, too. Sometimes we say things for certain times and then adapt them for others. And I'm okay with that.

As a life coach, I observe incongruities and inconsistencies as part of the process of naming "our stuff" in order to point us toward places for growth. Everyone has at least one truly deep story that has defined them (positively or not) and when life presents a new narrative, the possibilities can be transformative!

Think of Moses at the bush, Saul on Damascus road, Nelson Mandela in prison.

I said above that there are few absolutes. One of these is that you are not finished with your story yet. I have an amazing aunt who is ninety-two and very much "alive 'n well." Just the other night she was smiling, laughing and appreciating that 25 of us in the family just Zoomed with her. Or there's Sal who, at the same age of ninety-one, published his fourth book.... oh, and by the way, he also narrated it for Audible.

This is not to say necessarily that you have to be productive or technologically savvy. But during these crazy times isn't it nicer to be surprised by life rather than focusing on what or who is disappointing?

Gore Vidal once wrote, "Since no one can ever know for certain whether or not his own view of life is the correct one, it is absolutely impossible for him to know if someone else's is the wrong one."

My Mom had it correct both ways: "Be presentable" and "God doesn't mind how you look."

Daniel Francis

What You Are Made For

When I was in college, one of my classmates shared the
fact that he suffered from Seasonal Affective Disorder
(S.A.D.). For years, as autumn turned to winter his moods
would swing, his energy would sap and he'd have low-
grade depression. Some people talk about the "winter
blues", a seasonal funk that kidnaps motivation or
displaces energy. For sure, dark late-afternoons that limit
time outside can deprive you of Vitamin D, outdoor
exercise, gardening or other COVID-safe experiences.

Maybe this is why Christmas lights, decorated trees and
holiday TV specials get us in a good mood- they
counterbalance the gloomier feelings.

But unless you are sidelined by these feelings, what if you
took the time and created the space to listen to them? I
hope you know feelings won't kill you, even if they could
disturb you; sometimes inner disturbance isn't a bad thing:
it often offers vital information.

C.S. Lewis once wrote:

> You have stood before some landscape, which
> seems to embody what you have been looking for
> all your life … All the things that have deeply
> possessed your soul have been but hints of it–
> tantalizing glimpses, promises never quite fulfilled,
> echoes that died away just as they caught your ear.
> But if it should really become manifest– if there
> ever came an echo that did not die away but
> swelled into the sound itself–you would know it.
> Beyond all possibility of doubt you would say
> "Here at last is the thing I was made for."

Rather than a dark, dreary disposition, experiencing the
fullness of this season could open up all sorts of

possibilities and opportunities. Hear the echo from your deepest, truest self- a place that is always filled with the most brilliant light and sacred goodness.

That's the place where there can never be SADness nor meanness.

Negativity is ultimately incompatible with the truest you. Know this and live this.

Daniel Francis

10,000 Steps

"Will you get your steps in today?"

"Did you get a badge?"

"What was your average HR during your walk?"

If you don't understand these questions, you probably don't have a smartwatch or fitness tracker. We don't either, but we do get our miles in every day. For us, launching Alive 'n Well involves literally "walking the walk." Except for the occasional all-day rain, lunch hour finds us outside to get our steps in- either walking, running or biking: usually around 3 miles. Saturdays we go for more than 6.

The now sacred bar of "getting in your 10,000 steps" has its origins in a Japanese company that invented a device in 1965 called Manpo-kei, which translates to "10,000 steps meter" (there are crazy stories of competition among fitness fakes who have put their watch/trackers on dogs, blenders or fan blades to inflate their numbers).

But whether you're doing your 10K steps for bragging rights or bolstering your immune system, what I like about walking is that it gets us outside into *unconditioned* air: time to admire lawns and gardens; wave to neighbors and other walkers; look for hawks; listen for the great-horned owl; smell gardenias and jasmine; identify planets and stars. It's so good to stretch our legs after time at our desks; it is said that too much sitting is the new smoking.

Before I met my wife, much of my outdoor time was dedicated to getting in my running. Do you remember the Walkman (I still have one) that played a cassette tape (I do not have any)? How about the fact that the name of the product was telling us to get moving! Love it. So I say to you: walkwoman, walkman! If you can and are able, get outside and move your legs. It's not only good for your body but also refreshing for your mind.

Nietzsche once said, "It is only ideas gained from walking that have any worth." Thoreau, another avid walker, claimed, "The moment my legs begin to move my thoughts begin to flow." So, if you don't like the outdoors (heat, skeeters, the virus, sidewalk cracks and other obstacles), then walk indoors: plug in the treadmill; go up and down the stairs or just one step; walk around the couch or kitchen.

Get moving.

Daniel Francis

[Don't] Hear Ye! [Don't] Hear Ye!

There's a precious scene early in the movie *It's a Wonderful Life* whereby young Mary whispers into little George's deaf ear: "Is this the ear you can't hear on? George Bailey, I'll love you till the day I die." Even though she knew he couldn't hear her, she meant it and proved it by waiting, being strong and standing by him in his greatest need.

My wife and I are intentional about not wading into the murky morass of politics on our website and social media feeds. It's not that we don't have personal opinions and strong feelings; it's that we want Alive 'n Well to be a space that sows unity more than discord.

That being said, something we read about the late Supreme Court Justice Ruth Bader Ginsburg struck us as helpful, no matter what your political persuasion. It was an interview from four years ago when she revealed some good advice:

> It comes from my savvy mother-in-law, advice she gave me on my wedding day. "In every good marriage," she counseled, "it helps sometimes to be a little deaf." I have followed that advice assiduously, and not only at home through 56 years of a marital partnership nonpareil. I have employed it as well in every workplace, including the Supreme Court. When a thoughtless or unkind word is spoken, best tune out. Reacting in anger or annoyance will not advance one's ability to persuade.

What's the takeaway? We don't need to react to anything. We can choose to respond. Do you see the difference? The first is an impulse that might have us do/say/email/tweet/post something regrettable.

The second--always after a pause which draws from truth,

strength and honesty--will consistently align with the best and highest in us.

It's not so much that we are being deaf (or blind or dumb); rather, we are choosing carefully and kindly what we hear (or see or understand).

If you have a case of knee-jerk reactions, may it be dismissed!

Daniel Francis

Velcro and Teflon

We heard the adage perhaps when we were young: "Sticks and stones may break my bones, but names will never hurt me." It conveys an important lesson about knowing your inner strength and self-love. But with suicide due to bullying and online trolling, the message does not get received or believed. Offensive texts can hurt and cause a lot of suffering- sometimes even death.

Back when I was a kid if someone said something unkind to you, it stung... but the insults of the bully soon echoed away and Ajax or Comet cleaned whatever malicious message marked your locker door.

Nowadays, however, memes and mean posts live in cyberspace forever.

There was another playground phrase we employed to defend ourselves from a verbal tyrant: "I'm rubber and you are glue; everything you say bounces off of me and sticks to you!" It had a nice rhyming technique, no?

Among others, we have two powerful tools: Teflon and Velcro.

At times it's good to be "non-stick" and merely notice what's going on without reacting (or posting) which only compounds negative feelings.

At other times, it's good to let things "cling" to you: the spangle of autumn, the text pic of a newborn infant, the sound of an old song or new catchy tune, the scent of leaves, the redness of Mars in the night sky, a cute bumper sticker, the taste of homemade pizza or freshly baked cookies, the feel of water showering your body after yardwork or a run.

Is it too morbid to ask: At the end of our lives, will we want to be nursing old wounds or just blessedly grateful for having been PRESENT to many beautiful moments?

Take a look this afternoon and this weekend: what do you choose to cling to and what can you let go of?

Daniel Francis

Where There Is Darkness, Light

People from all walks of life and from many religious traditions honor the holy man whose feast day is today, October 4: Giovanni di Pietro di Bernardone, known to us as St. Francis- a poor man with a wealth of wisdom and practical spirituality from the town of Assisi, Italy.

To relegate his memory to mere garden statues or quaint hagiography does not do justice to this man and his legacy.

Born into a wealthy family, he experienced a profound conversion after serving in the army and recovering from an illness. Becoming an ardent follower of Christ, the charismatic young man embraced a life of profound simplicity, unitive prayer and exemplary love of the poor. His 500-year-old spirituality bequeaths to us a contemporary reverence for creation, particularly our climate and natural resources.

Perhaps St. Francis' greatest legacy--and one which is needed right now in our country and throughout the world--is his commitment to peace.

One could write volumes on each of the lines of the Peace Prayer which is attributed to the saint. However, due to the enormous challenges and realities of this year, the line which speaks to me is "Where there is darkness, light."

Covid-19 came to us in the winter darkness of this year (for those who live in the northern hemisphere). It brought with it many things: uncertainty, hoarding, fear, blame, toxic racism with impassioned protests and violence, along with massive financial stress. The virus also carried with it a death warrant for too many as well as the suffering and mourning for those who witnessed the same.

And yet through all of this, and because of all of this was born--and continues to grow--a sense of responsibility, compassion, cooperation, inventiveness, spontaneity and social outreach the likes of which I cannot remember in my lifetime.

I may be called out of touch or Pollyannas, but one thing (among many) that we know and believe and try to live is that *how you see is what you see*- meaning that our attitude toward the world is greatly determined by the world that we have created within. We choose, in the craziness and unsteadiness of this time, to bring light as we can, how we can, when we can.

We do not claim to do this perfectly or always.

With the tumult of national politics and dis-ease of international unrest, there are times we have to coach each other back into the place and space where we drink of the truth of the goodness of life. For that reason, we subscribe to the proverb that "It's better to light one candle than to curse the darkness."

Indeed, these are the moments that call for light. There's enough roller-coastering of emotions in "normal times". Disrupted lives, worry, loneliness, disorganization and just not-knowing can take its toll. But where there is darkness, we can bring light.

Perhaps just to pause and think differently about a situation. Perchance it's re-prioritizing and really making someone or something matter.

Maybe your comfort zone is making you uncomfortable? Good. Take a breath and find out if you have "stinking thinking" and, if you do, discover--however you can--that unlimited source of light within that was planted by someone other than you.

Take a breath and make the time to change up the daily rituals that govern your life.

Or affirm the ones you know are working for you. Either way, throw yourself into them as if your health and life were at stake... they are.

And if you've been wondering where to draw inspiration, read or pray the following:

> Lord, make me an instrument of your peace,
> Where there is hatred, let me sow love;
> Where there is injury, pardon;
> Where there is doubt, faith;
> Where there is despair, hope;
> Where there is darkness, light;
> Where there is sadness, joy; O Divine Master,
> Grant that I may not so much seek
> To be consoled as to console;
> To be understood as to understand;
> To be loved as to love. For it is in giving that we receive;
> It is in pardoning that we are pardoned;
> And it is in dying that we are born to eternal life.

St. Francis is more than someone to admire; he is a person to imitate.

I read somewhere that in the presence of a man or woman in whom all hostility has died, others cannot be hostile. In the presence of a woman or man in whom fear is no more, no one can be afraid.

This is the power released in divine serenity, as we can see in the life of San Francisco. Because all hostility had died in his heart, he was a profound force for peace.

Perhaps this Day of St. Francis inspires you to "do more."

Don't Hold Back

Often on one of our walking routes, my wife and I see a dog in the yard. He's curious and sometimes barks while wagging his tail. He'll move with us- we on the street and he along the grass. But the dog never leaves the yard. Is there an invisible/electric fence? Is he well-trained? Could he not be bothered?

Did you ever hear of The Baby Elephant Principle? Basically, it's the idea that an immature elephant--tied to a stake while growing up--will think that it can't move even when there is no longer a stake or rope present.

Similarly, there was an experiment done in the last century whereby pike fish living in a tank were separated from minnows by a glass plate. After a while, the pike had bumped into the glass partition so often that they stopped going after the minnows, even after the partition was removed.

Are you stuck in the "same ol' same ol'" thinking? What are the (in)visible ropes or partitions that keep you from taking the next step?

Let me ask another question: do you know what your "next step" is?

> An exercise regimen
> A (new) job Retirement Cleaning up that "oh my God!" room
> Talking with your doctor
> Beginning--or finishing--that project

If you hold back your true, next step it's like not dealing with what's going on inside.

As a friend of mine learned when going through recovery,

"When you bury your feelings, they are buried alive."
They will, in a sense, haunt you until they find healthy
expression in a constructive channel.

So who or what is holding you back?   If you think you can
or cannot... you are correct.

Positively Speaking

When Alice and I began to make our home together, we went through the collective stuff we brought along. Alice's mother had passed away not long before and we had her stuff in a closet- old cookbooks, quilter's magazines, postcards and meticulously detailed financial records. Then we saw a box that was labeled "old negatives." I knew what they were- those strips of celluloid that accompanied photos the store developed for you (remember that we actually had to wait a week to have our Kodak moments processed?).

But I got to thinking- how many "old negatives" do we carry around? Moments in time that stand still: being bullied in 4th grade, overlooked by family when we did something extraordinary, decades-old disagreements... so many snarled snapshots of the past when an argument, break-up or accusation was transferred onto our mind's canvas... and whenever a thought, memory, smell or emotion brings it up, the curtains open and the drama is re-played.

THERE'S A DIFFERENT WAY TO LIVE

What if we learned to cultivate "new positives"? Imagine if we had a mantra for tough days that went something like, "This is only how my life looks like now..." Is it possible for you to think forward, have a future memory and just know that your life is beginning to look like you want it?

Wouldn't it be much more life-giving to have <u>new positives</u> beckon you onward rather than define yourself by the crippled story of old negatives?

The late Anthony DeMello writes:

Imagine that you're unwell and in a foul mood, and they're taking you through some lovely countryside. The landscape is beautiful but you're not in the mood to see anything. A few days later you pass the same place and you say, "Good heavens, where was I that I didn't notice all of this"? Everything becomes beautiful when you change. Or you look at the trees and the mountains through windows that are wet with rain from a storm, and everything looks blurred and shapeless. You want to go right out there and change those trees, change those mountains. Wait a minute, let's examine your window. When the storm ceases and the rain stops, and you look out the window, you say, "Well, how different everything looks". We see people and things not as they are, but as we are.

That is why when two people look at something or someone, you get two different reactions.

We see things and people not as they are, but as we are.

Put this program into action, a thousand times:

- identify the negative feelings in you;
- understand that they are in you, not in the world, not in external reality;
- do not see them as an essential part of "I"; these things come and go;
- understand that when you change, everything changes.

Soul Food

I'm re-reading Annie Dillard's *For the Time Being*. You're not going to find odder works of non-fiction and yet I come back to so many of the images in her book. Part poet, part mystic, she writes:

> Ours is a planet sown in beings. Our generations overlap like shingles. We don't fall in rows like hay, but we fall. Once we get here, we spend forever on the globe, most of it tucked under. While we breathe, we open time like a path in the grass. We open time as a boat's stem slits the crest of the present. and There is no less holiness at this time- as you are reading this- than there was on the day the Red Sea parted.

Dillard weaves into the story the thoughts of Jesuit paleontologist, Pierre Teilhard de Chardin who wrote that "we are not human beings having a spiritual experience; we are spiritual beings having a human experience."

If this is true, then becoming a spiritual person cannot be reduced merely to tips, techniques, and a certain posture... as helpful as these may be. It's not even really about a religious experience or a holy feeling. Spirituality is the attentiveness between our soul and the Spirit of God. It's about coming home to our humanity.

In our DNA is the desire—no, the need!—to connect with something bigger than ourselves and life can teach us that it's right here in so many ways.

So how do you become a spiritual person?

That's the problem- you and I, we don't really *become* anything. You let something emerge in you.

61

It's an active attentiveness- an awareness of what has always, already been with and in you; if you will, it's a soul resuscitation.

Some authors use the phrase "monkey mind" to describe the crazy dramas we often create when we lose consciousness. The opposite of monkey mind is mature spirituality.

See if this sounds familiar:

> When you take the time to reflect on something beautiful, simple, stunning or inspirational, you're being spiritual

> When you ponder deeply something that occurs to you from a place of profound truth and knowing, you're being spiritual

> When you think seriously about the highest values in your life, whether you're at a crossroads or while you're sailing smoothly, you're accessing what's called spiritual.

> Whenever your mind moves away from the frantic and frenetic, when the ego stops bossing you around and you stop the "stinking thinking" of the monkey mind, then you're living on the level of the spiritual

You're a spiritual person. Be aware of your depth and let it start seeping OUT of you.

Seriously.

Watch it happen. You cannot help but be even more intentional when you realize how spiritual you already are!

GPS

For eighteen years I traveled a lot. If it hadn't been for the GPS navigation technology in my car, I'd still be looking for the off-ramp to St. Mary's Church in Peoria, IL.

You hear people say at times to "pay attention to the details" and "notice the small stuff." This is true. But I've also determined that there are generally two buckets into which you can put most of life's lessons. I have named these buckets GPS, or Gratitude Plus Surrender.

Think about it... so much of what we experience each day is a gift. Just the fact that we awoke and our heart and lungs had remembered to do their thing during the night. The morning coffee and our breakfast. The joy of an unexpected text or snail mail. Perhaps an exercise routine or meditation discipline. All of these fit nicely in the bucket called Gratitude.

But what happens when something outside our control affects us negatively?

What do you do with bad news, a small hiccup or major disaster? That's when we place it into the bucket, Surrender. Surrender does not mean "give up" or "give in." It merely serves as a way to name an experience before it can maim us mentally. Remember: how you think is how you live. The way you regard something, someone, anything is the way you regard life!

So yes, make time to enjoy the small stuff and all the beautiful details of daily life. But remember to take notes when the Big Lessons come your way.

We've all been there. It's a whirlwind of emotions and directions. Where to go? Whom to ask? What to do? How to behave?

Daniel Francis

The answers to these questions are your decisions, your choices. No one forces you to feel things or go a certain way. The more intentionally you respond to life's unpleasant surprises, the more you direct life to go the way you want it to.

If you lose your way, use your GPS: gratitude plus surrender.

Look Ahead

Have you ever experienced the frustration associated with installing a computer or smartphone update which touts improvements and "fixes", only to find out it's maddeningly difficult to get accustomed to and navigate? Apple and Microsoft often want us to upgrade the software versions of our hardware.

All this leads me to ask, What version of your life are you on? Come on- you can't still be living out of the version you were when you were a child or teenager or even young adult? For sure there are tones and hues from those days, but you have radically changed.

So...what "fixes" have chiseled you to be the person you are now? What are you still working on?

Carl Jung once wrote, "You are what you do, not what you tell me you do." Are you living your best life now? Is your operating system set on the highest volume of Integrity and Passion?

Cheryl Richardson, life coach and best-selling author, says that your mission is not where you currently are, but where you want to be.

Whenever I watch basketball or soccer I'm impressed when a player simultaneously does three things while on the move: controls the ball, evades a defender and-- because he snatches glimpses of the playing field in front of him--knows which teammate he'll eventually pass to. His eye is on a goal, but the next smartest move might be to give it to someone else.

To be a good player you have to have a wide view, determination and patience.

Daniel Francis

What are your goals? What have you been kicking around these past few years? What would be your next move and why? As we say adieu to 2020, take a moment and ask these questions.

Remember: if you don't act on life (choose what YOU want to do), then life will certainly act on you. Isn't it true? How often do we let someone else's mood or another driver's carelessness change us? Why do we give away our peace so easily? And what can we do to maintain peace in the face of circumstances that challenge it?

The first step is to recognize the fact that we're dealing on the level of thought. And then to realize: I can choose to think differently despite how I feel. Once you recognize this freedom, you can write the script of how your day will go.

Years ago, perhaps on a gloomy day, Robert Frost penned these words:

> The way a crow
> Shook down on me
> The dust of snow
> From a hemlock tree
> Has given my heart
> A change of mood
> And saved some part
> Of a day I had rued.

Imagine if the pandemic and craziness of this year changes us, awakens us to be the best version of ourselves?

What's In Your Oven?

There's something about summer that slows us down.
Perhaps it's the heat! or the longer days so you don't feel
rushed before dark? or maybe it's the memories of
yesteryear when summertime was playtime- you slept late,
did a chore or two and then only checked in at home base
to cram down a meal before more kick-the-can, baseball or
tree climbing.

Ah, those halcyon days of adolescence.

In my practice as a Life Coach, I hear people who crave
the past as if living "there" could change their mood. And
it might, but only for an instant. How we live now is the
way we'll live tomorrow.

But here's the secret: if you have a plan, line up
possibilities, keep a calendar for ideas and dreams, you
always have something to look forward to.

I remember the first time I heard a pregnant woman refer
to her bump as "a bun in the oven." It sounded offensive
or, at the least, disrespectful, until she continued, "My
body is like a timer set for 4 1/2 more months."

I'll never know how it feels to be pregnant, but I can say
that I've had that fertile feeling of creativity and
expectation. Whether it's buying a paint set and knowing
it's for a rainy day or the eagerness of watching a movie
whose trailer I've been seeing for months, there's
something about holding the promise now of a future
possession.

Think about it: When you have tickets in your hand for a
concert or sports event, they're merely pieces of cellulose
wood pulp we call paper, but they give us access to
tremendous joy. A small metallic key is not the car but it

Daniel Francis

literally opens the door to our "wheels." A ring in a felt
box means nothing without the love and commitment
signified by the giver's smile and bended knee. You get
the idea.

Knowing what we have and holding the promise of
possibility is to have a "bun in the oven." There's
something to look forward to, grow into, or become
identified with.

So whether you have vaccinated vacation plans this
summer or not, schedule something now for August or
October. It doesn't have to be expensive.

Get it on your calendar.

Put it under that magnet on your fridge.

What you imagine in your mind becomes real only when
you set it in motion. You might have every thought about
baking a cake, but unless you get Pillsbury from Publix, the
idea is merely quaint and utterly unfulfilled.

If you're not good to yourself, what or whom are you
waiting for?

Up or Down

An elderly friend called some time ago. Recently, because of stability issues, Patrick relies on the help of a cane. He told me that the nurse had to instruct him by saying, "Don't look down when you walk!"

It must be quite a change: 80 years walking without assistance, putting one foot in front of the other... and you wake up one day and have to learn to lean on a stick for mobility.

I can't remember the first time I skated, but I can imagine how often I looked down at my feet.

When my father took the training wheels off my bike, I was ecstatic; but I was apologetic and embarrassed when I slammed into the back bumper of a parked car on the street because I was looking down.

Someone who appears sad might be asked, "Why are you looking so down?"

When I was taking counseling classes, some fellow students would make fun of psychology as "navel-gazing", or looking too much inwards. But perhaps there is some truth to that.

What I've learned from Life is that there is so much to miss if you don't look up and around.

Sure, there's a place and time for looking down (at your self) and behind (where you've come from).

But life is so full of teachers and lessons, gifts and surprises, new experiences and constant reminders... looking down can--well--get you down!

The ostrich may never see unpleasantness, but she doesn't

Daniel Francis

see reality either.

A wise teacher once wrote: "How you see is what you
see." Do you see? If not, look up!

Another First

I heard it said that failure is simply early attempts at success.

It's important to realize that what we learn from our failures can be important stepping stones.

Listen to some of the experts:

> "No pressure, no diamonds." -Mary Case

> "I have not failed; I have just found 10,000 ways that don't work." -Thomas Edison

> "Failure is just the opportunity to begin again; this time more intelligently." -Henry Ford

> "It's not that I'm so smart; I just stay with the problems longer." -Albert Einstein

> "When you are going through hell... keep going!" - Winston Churchill

When we train ourselves to look at "failures" as learning experiences and course corrections, obstacles become teachers and setbacks are part of the curriculum. Einstein said, "If I only have an hour to solve a problem, I will spend 55 minutes asking the right question and then 5 minutes solving the problem."

So what's the question you need to ask at this moment? What can get you from the life you are living now to the life you know you want to live? Do the "gremlins" taunt you that you can't or do you allow the limbic monkeys to rattle your mental cage with negativity? What's the best version of your life? Are you living it now? Why not?

New Year's Eve is exactly one month from now. The beginning of each month is a golden opportunity for us to take inventory of where we are, where we've come from and where we'd like to go (perhaps you've heard that "if you don't know where you're going, any road will get you there").

Last year I read *A Year to Live* by Stephen Levine (Bell Tower, 1997). Having been a hospice worker for many years, he accompanied the dying and knows the territory surrounding the last days of people's lives. So he embarked on a year-long experiment to "practice dying as the highest form of wisdom" (Socrates) and shared how such conscious living forces us to examine our priorities.

Regarding the subject of near-death occurrences, Levine writes: "Most who returned from such an experience came back with three very precious insights: an increased appreciation of life, a diminished fear of death, and a new sense of purpose."

So on this first of December, how do you want to start this last month of the year?

On the cusp of a new year, new decade...how can you learn from loss and gain some wisdom in the process?

A Positive Virus

Not to worry, neither of us has been infected with COVID- and we hope that's the case for a long time. But this disease and the pandemic which rages on is one of the principal reasons why Alice and I began this initiative, Alive 'n Well.

However, well before the world became conversant with terms such as co-morbidity, R0 ("R Naught"), herd immunity or contact tracing, we've had a desire--perhaps you could even call it a mission--to help others in the way we can.

Switching gears for a moment... Have you noticed this where you live: a sofa or tricycle left on the curb or driveway with a "4 Free" sign? The other day, we saw a broadcast spreader for the taking- you know, the non-motorized lawn utility that helps to diffuse seeds and fertilizer?

It got me thinking about the persuasive super-spreaders of goodness. The honorable teachers, influencers, motivational people who live and breathe positivity and hope. Sometimes spiritual, but never superficial, these women and men seem to have a mission to share what they know from what they've experienced with whoever is eager to learn.

Let me be clear about content: I don't mean the stuff that is sappy, pie-in-the-sky, groundless nice talk. That's what I call junk food (whereas I call negativity **poison**- both of which do nothing to nourish).

No- super-spreaders are those people who have this way of circulating a deeper, broader truth that is available to all; it's just that some of us have buried it under the clutter of drama or the junk of defeat.

Daniel Francis

Years ago I learned from Richard Rohr that what I don't transform I transmit. Meaning: the world can, at times, infect us with a heavy sadness.

Consequently, we have a choice: to contaminate others OR let it pass through and return it with a twist: life is always better than the darkest day; hope is never beaten down to stay.

The Placid Lake

There's a lake not too far from our house. My wife and I love to walk there and do so nearly daily. If we have old bread we feed it to the fish, turtles and occasional seagull or crow. Oftentimes, there is no one there at the little beach or on the boardwalk.

When there are no boaters and the wind is holding its breath, the hush of the water mirrors the sky above as well as the houses and trees on the other side of the lake.

It reminds me of my many years "up north" where the temperatures froze the pond water for us college students to skate or play hockey. There was a solid stillness that made the ice seem as if it were a mirage.

What's real and not merely a mirage is that the calmer you are inside, the more you are able to reflect back that stillness outside of you. In 2004 I went on sabbatical and spent a month in a cabin in upstate New York. Perhaps I was trying to channel my inner Henry David Thoreau, but there were whole days when I was able to sit, meditate, be still and just notice things. I suppose if someone saw me they might have perceived a man "wasting time." I'll admit it was a luxury few people have or use. What was not a waste was trying to whittle away the parts of me that had become fragmented and couldn't find a place to fit-churning waters which betrayed unsettled depths.

One day, sitting on the porch after scrumptious porridge, I spied a black bear at most two hundred yards away. For 30 minutes, either not smelling me (they have poor eyesight) or not caring, the bear loped along in its own world nibbling berries by the stream. And then--as quickly as it came into view--it disappeared into the thicket.

Don't you find that, when you take the time to stop and be

Daniel Francis

still or just slow down and pause with a cup of coffee or
slice of apple, you're better able to see beyond the morass
of chaos into the ordinary, beautiful--sometimes
shockingly simple--exhilarations of just living and
breathing?

Behind the Masks

Halloween is tomorrow night. Children may or may not
be trick-or-treating, depending on your local ordinances or
parents' directives. Maybe it's me, but it seems as if people
were more than artful in putting up decorations this year-
and they started earlier than ever.

Most of us are used to the macabre recreations of zombies,
mummies and front yard cemeteries. I have a particular
appreciation for the more creative epitaphs, such as "I told
you I was sick" or "Here lies an atheist all dressed up and
no place to go" or my newest favorite "Don't make me
come up there!"

Where we shop for groceries, we know or at least
recognize most of the employees. With their masks on,
you can still see them smiling by the squint or gleam in
their eyes.

Similarly, when I talk to a customer representative by
phone, I can hear their patience with me and joy when the
issue is resolved (or the opposite!).

Once, when I was too old for trick-or-treating but still
gluttonous for Goobers, I donned my younger sister's
Casper the Friendly Ghost mask and went down the street.
It didn't fool Mrs. Sheehan, but she still gave me some
candy.

"Mask" comes from the word to cover up or fool; mascara
is a related concept.

No one can fool Covid and you can't ultimately cheat
death, despite the masks we wear outside and the ones we
sometimes wear on the inside.

But what we can do is look into the eyes, truly listen to the

Daniel Francis

voices of both the people we love and those with whom
we disagree.

Yes, I say this as we face not only All Hallow's Eve but
Election Eve.

Mars and Us

If you think the fourth planet from the sun is brighter these nights, you're not mistaken. The "Red Planet", as Mars is also called, is unmistakably touting its vermillion hue. Hurry, however: it won't be this close to our planet for another 15 years.

I'm reading a book by Bill Bryson called *A Short History of Nearly Everything*. It's funny and informative and, like so many of his other works, inspires me to be a better citizen of this planet. For example, I was fascinated to learn that we know more about the surface of Mars than we do about our ocean floor here on Earth.

Sometimes when I hear a news story of two countries fighting or a politician's problematic position or a negative statistic about COVID, the economy or joblessness, I feel like a Martian.

And yet the best in me knows that this terra incognita is my land, our land, even if we don't yet know precisely how to live on it with peace and fairness. Yet.

I heard recently that the definition of an optimist is someone who knows there is a solution. I like that.

Just as John F. Kennedy could see us walking on the moon even though he was dead before it happened, one day we'll look at Earth's oceans from the Red Planet and know there's still so much to discover- inside and out!

Daniel Francis

The World Seriously

I wouldn't call us fanatics, but my wife and I watch our share of sports. We root for the home teams and are particularly proud of our Tampa Bay Lightning and Rays. The other day we saw Tom Brady and Aaron Rodgers-- fierce opponents--embrace and smile after their game together, even though one of them lost to the other.

Wouldn't it be marvelous if nations could compete, as in the Olympics, but only in the sphere of strength, speed, poise and precision?

Not a few months after the 9/11 attacks, there was a play on Broadway called "The Guys" about Nick, a fire captain, who lost eight men in the collapse of the World Trade Center.

As he prepares for each eulogy, Nick gets help from a writer, Joan. A most touching point in the drama occurs when Joan begins to sob. Through the captain's stories, she has gotten to know these deceased men so well that she weeps for their deaths, the wives and lives and children they leave behind.

> Nick says, "I'm sorry. I shouldn't put you through all this sadness."

> Joan replies, "I want to hear this. No, I need to hear this. I need to know their stories. These are not just your guys. They were my brothers. I knew then that every time I saw a person on the street, I saw only his public shadow. The rest, the important part, lived in layer after layer beyond my view."

We have no idea what wonders are hidden in the people around us. Behind every mild or mean post, truthful or twisted tweet; behind every lawn sign promoting a candidate; behind the masks and smiles and frowns of every person we meet or see online or on TV is a multi-layered story.

Oh, we're going to continue watching sports, as trite as they may seem in comparison with what is happening "in the world"; and we're going to quietly differ from opinions we don't share; but we're cheering for a bright, inextinguishable torch that can be passed on to the next generation which assures them that they matter in all their hidden wonder: irrespective of political stripe or skin tone, dialect or accent, country of origin or religious leaning... these are our guys, our gals.

Daniel Francis

Blind Spot Detector

Growing up the sixth of 7 children, there was not a lot of alone time with Mom or Dad. Dental visits and afterschool activities all used the same Uber pool of chauffeur parents.

But the day I passed my driver's exam, it was Dad and I alone celebrating with lunch at Wendy's. He was proud of me and probably relieved and nervous as well- relieved because there was now only one more child that would need his patience for parallel parking; nervous, because now one more child would require prayers and summon fears when asked to "borrow the keys."

Years before getting behind the wheel of the car, one of the lessons I learned by watching and listening to my father was not to remain in another car's "blind spot."

In the 90s, when I lived in NYC I would often see the carriage tours in Central Park. That was the first time I noticed the blinders that horses wear to prevent them from getting "spooked" by visual distractions from the peripheries.

In this time in our country, perhaps we need to take off our myopic blinders to see wider and have a broader perspective.

Notice: I say "see" and not "agree" or "accept." That might not happen for a while--if ever--for some. But the "United" in these "States" depends on the majority of us seeing the best in us and not being spooked by differences.

Thankfully, many of us today drive cars that have "blind spot detectors"; when we pay attention, this technology can help us avoid a collision or worse.

Is there someone in your life that helps you with your blind spots? Do you ever read or listen outside of your bias? Are you able to just "see" another opinion without judgment, derision or outright rejection?

If yes, treat yourself to a meal at Wendy's once COVID is over.

Daniel Francis

Do It Now

Recently a classmate of my wife passed away. He had posted something very beautiful on Facebook just two days before. On the same day, we saw that Alex Trebek (the long-time host of Jeopardy!) had also died.

This month of November begins with All Hallow's Day (celebrating all the departed holy souls) and ends with Thanksgiving. Like bookmarks of this penultimate month, we are stirred to be grateful for those who have gone before us.

But perhaps we can also be grateful that we are still alive. Like Scrooge on the morning after, we thrust open the window sash and breath in new air and realize we still have time to do things, change things, re-think things and obtain more inner peace.

In the kitchen of my home when I was growing up was a plaque with a quote from Etienne de Grellet which read: "I shall pass this way but once; any good that I can do or any kindness I can show to any human being, let me do it now. Let me not defer nor neglect it, for I shall not pass this way again."

I doubt that Alice's classmate nor Alex Trebek were thinking of polls or politics or the pandemic when they were dying. You've heard it before but let's ask the question again: what if we lived today as if we might die tomorrow? How would that change our thoughts, words, choices and actions?

Good Neighbors

In our neighborhood, there are magnificent trees: oak, cypress, pine, elm, palm, maple among many others. You can't miss the sycamores, however: their plate-sized leaves float and fall everywhere.

I must confess the glee I get when channeling my inner child and tromping through the piles that gather spontaneously in the curb- think of the sound of crushing a bag of potato chips and you're a few decibels short.

Three years ago Senator Paul Rand's ribs were broken when he had a fight with his neighbor over grass clippings and leaves. This reminds me of Robert Frost's poem with the line "Good fences make good neighbors." [As an aside, in the poem Frost didn't agree and wanted to remove the stone wall that separated their lands.]

Back to sycamore leaves... to see them blown all down the block makes me wonder how neighbors deal with this yearly arboreal jetsam. Do they, like I, love the sight of this stately tree enough to endure the interloping debris... or do they pray for borer beetles to bring the sycamore down after enough eating?

Just before the election, I heard that a supporter of X found out his neighbor's sign (for Y) had been stolen. Despite the fact that they disagreed politically, he went out and purchased a replacement sign for Y- not his own candidate.

All of this to ask: what do we do with the winds (ill or chill) that blow our way? What if that which disturbs or challenges us can actually make us stronger?

Daniel Francis

Thanksgiving- the Day After

I'm writing this before Thanksgiving. It scheduled to "drop" Friday.

Perhaps some of you will need to drop as well- after shopping, prepping, cleaning, baking, waking up early to start the oven, cooking, entertaining, texting and calling, playing touch football, washing lots of dishes and then dessert and after-dinner drinks and stories!

Our hope is that you all stayed safe. Maybe some of you-- such as our Francis family--scheduled a Zoom meeting to see everybody's faces. The gift of technology never ceases to amaze!

Black Friday is mainly online. I don't know how it got that name, but my opinion is that it gave Thanksgiving a black eye. I remember relatives that quite literally left warm turkey on the table to stand and wait in line for "door-busting" sales.

What I know to be true is that thanksgiving doesn't stop after the turkey (or lasagna in our house) is eaten. We awake grateful for many things too numerous to name here.

We don't quit our attitude of gratitude even in the face of bad or sad news, for our giving thanks is independent of outside circumstances.

When we know this and live out of this, everything changes!

Gravy's Gone, Gratitude Goes On

It's eight days after Thanksgiving. Perhaps you're now sick of turkey until 2021 or that pumpkin pie miraculously has one more slice with your name on it. More and more decorations are accenting houses and yards in our neighborhood. It feels as if mid-November through New Years could be one combined holiday called Thankmaseve.

Just as chocolate on February 14th or May roses for mom are tokens of a love that transcends those special days, Thanksgiving also invites us to magnify an attitude that is, at heart, a fundamental choice: to see the good and right every day- in March as well as November.

Yes, things go wrong and people die (especially this year) and there are tragedies aplenty- some of which are avoidable. But it's our decision to name and voice at least some of the hundreds of positive things that happen daily rather than nurse the festering wounds of what is going wrong, what can't be fixed or what is beyond our control.

It's no surprise that grateful people are happy people. On the other hand, those who see the glass half-empty are never content.

It reminds me of an old joke about a doting granny who takes her eight-year-old grandson to the beach.

> A giant wave comes crashing in and sweeps the little boy out to sea. She looks up at the heavens and pleads, "God, please. He's my only grandson. I love him more than life itself. Please, bring him back to me."

> Suddenly, the waters part as if they were the Red Sea. A ray of light shines from the sky. She sees a golden dolphin heading toward the shore with

Daniel Francis

little Jimmy on his back. The dolphin gently places her grandson on the beach, then swims away toward a beautiful rainbow.

The old woman looks at her grandson, gazes around the beach and finally raises her eyes to God and exclaims, "He had a hat."

Heaven on Earth

On the night before my mom died, the family was having supper together at my sister's house. Dad loved family and the more around the table the merrier! Although I wasn't there, I saw the video of my father raising a glass of wine and toasting everyone. He was so happy that he ended the toast with "It's like I died and went to heaven."

The next day's sadness was a gut punch. It was like hell on earth to lose Mom.

Why do I write all this on Christmas day?

Those of us born and raised in a Christian tradition celebrate today the birth of God's son, the Savior of the world: Jesus. His nativity is marked by gifts, wise men, the star, an angel and quaking shepherds. But the shadow of the cross falls even on this day: Joseph and Mary were denied hospitality, the son was born in an undignified cattle trough, poor and in a country ruled by despised foreigners.

And yet in the darkest part of the year (at least in the northern hemisphere), unto us a light shines. It's as if an opening in heaven revealed a way through the morass of hopelessness.

Not by abandoning earth but by embracing the heavenly here: Joseph stays with his pregnant wife; the shepherds go back home "a different way"; the vulnerability of a naked infant betokens the power and presence of God who says through a centurion 33 years later at another uninviting place, Calvary:

"Surely, this was the Messiah."

My dad was right- on the best of days we get a glimpse of

heaven. But we haven't died yet and there's still lots of work to do.

Maybe this season of Christmas will help us find heaven on earth in the little and large things that are the gifts of our life.

Merry Christmas!

"I Received That"

During this time of gift-giving, who of us doesn't recall
Christmases of yore. As Alice and I decorated our tree the
other day, we reminded one another of the stories behind
some of the ornaments: there's the tiny, covered bridge
we picked up in Vermont; that one was made by your
Mom; this was from our third year together...

My brother Jim often recounts a Christmas story from
when we were all young. The gifts for us seven children
were brought in one by one in large bags and laid at our
feet. Amidst the sounds of paper ripping and boxes
crunching, we were all oohing and awwing others' toys, as
was Jim. But then he began to cry. Apparently, each child
had received their bag of gifts... except for him. He could
only sustain happiness for the rest of us for so long until
the dam burst and disappointment tears began to flow.
Then Mom looked at Dad and realized one bag had yet to
be retrieved from their secret (Santa) storage. Soon
sadness turned to gladness and all was calm in the bright
Francis house.

Not too long ago, NBC's Hoda Kotb related what
happened when she complimented an assistant on work
she had done. The assistant looked at her and said, "I
received that." Hoda writes: "Her phrase 'I received that'
meant to me, 'What you've said to me is inside of me now.
I'm not deflecting it, I'm receiving it. I accept your kind
gift.'"

The response in Spanish and French to "Thank you"
translates literally to "It's nothing" (de nada; de rien). But
receiving a compliment well or expressing gratitude for a
gift is *something*- it expresses an inner strength that reveals a
truth often missing in verbal exchange: I am hearing you;
I'm listening; I'm receiving what you're saying and not
judging it. I'm not taking your side because this is not

91

about who's right- I'm listening to you and receiving what you are saying to me; and that's what I would want you to do for me, too. This is not nothing; this is certainly something very important in communication.

In a year when there has been a lot taken from us (normalcy, freedom, people we have loved and lost), please do not overlook the MANY gifts that come your way every day, but especially the ones that might come wrapped, stamped, delivered and opened by you on or around December 25th.

Practice thanking someone by saying "I received that" and really mean it.

Wisdom from a Lame Fox

Earlier this year, I had the joy and honor of assisting an elderly man write what could be his final book. In it, he reflects on his life, the lessons he's learned and how the reader can "enter eternity with ease" by allowing the ego to die.

Another book that has caught my attention is just out. The actor Michael J. Fox provides a pre-Thanksgiving gift that is a cornucopia of sage advice and poignant perspective.

In his memoir, we get a glimpse into the way Fox deals with Parkinson's Disease- it's like seeing a "disability" through a different prism.

Here's a slice of his life and perhaps, as you read this, you may be inspired--as I was--to be grateful for the gift of life and health that we so often take for granted:

> But what I'm only now starting to fully understand is that this is an inside job. It only works if I believe. I've always been confident, positive, doggedly determined; but doubt is beginning to mitigate my conviction. Who am I to think I can accomplish this, when so many have struggled with similar setbacks; some with Parkinson's, some with the aftermath of spinal surgery? I may be the only one who has taken on this particular two-headed beast... I have to learn to walk again; to reclaim my mobility, remaster my motion. I consider this fundamental to my therapy — for me, it all starts and ends with walking. And I understand that it's more complicated than that.
>
> So many tiny disciplines have to be observed, and neglected muscles and ligaments need to be

restored. I'm exhausted by the effort I've already put in at Johns Hopkins, and daunted by how much work I still have to do. It's like being nibbled to death by ducks.

Back in the days of carefree ambling, I would have considered the topic of walking to be rather pedestrian. Now the acts of stepping, strolling, hiking, and perambulating have become an obsession. I watch Esmé gliding through the kitchen, grabbing an apple while opening the fridge door for a coconut water, closing it with a quick shift of her hip and pirouetting out the swinging door at the other end of the room. Down in the lobby, my neighbor and her daughter are quickstepping to catch a taxi. I spy on a man walking with a slight limp, which he counterbalances with a bag of groceries. I secretly watch the way they all move.

Easy, breezy, catlike, or with a limp, every one of them is far better at it than me. It may be that the most difficult, miraculous thing we do, physically, is to walk.

-Michael J. Fox,
No Time Like the Future: An Optimist Considers Mortality
(Flatiron Books, November 17, 2020)

How Do You Define A Year?

As we make our way to the edge of this calendar year, there's so much to reflect back on during the 525,600 minutes that make up 2020. Who of us could have imagined--even in our wildest nightmares--that a world-wide virus would change the face of the earth (and make us cover our faces in public)? Think about it for a moment: something so tiny has killed 1.6 million people worldwide. A single human hair can hide 500 virus particles.

To the scary stew of pandemic, mix in powerful protests, contested elections, a teetering economy and it's easy to despair. And yet... We have experienced so much else this year: there have been births and bar mitzvahs, proposals and car parades, online graduations, amazing home baking prowess, ingenious ways of keeping in touch with our loved ones, new technology learned, the kindness of strangers and the compassion of many front-line and essential workers, not to mention neighbors who became Samaritans and others who pitched in.

In the stage production, *Rent*, a song is sung called "Seasons of Love". Here are some of the lyrics:

Five hundred twenty five thousand six hundred minutes
How do you measure a year?
In daylights, in sunsets, in midnights,
In cups of coffee,
In inches, in miles, in laughter, in strife
How do you measure a year in a life?
How about love?
How do you measure a life of a woman or a man?
In truths that she learned
Or in times that she cried
In bridges he burned
Or the way that she died

95

Daniel Francis

Its time now to sing out
The story never ends
Remember the love... How do you measure a year?

Are you able to celebrate the few amazing moments?
Watch yourself if you let anything negative define you.
Your source is sacred and your destiny is divine. In
between these two is your truth- the deepest, most
precious you is love. Remember this into 2021.

On The Cusp Of 2021

We laughed

We cried

We zoomed

We baked

We missed

We gained

WE MADE IT!

They say that "hindsight is 20/20" What is clear is that without a positive vision things can look blurry or even scary. On these last days of 2020 let's look back and say THANKS for what "distance learning" has taught us and say YES to what the new year will bring.

You can't choose your teachers: Mrs. Jones in 2nd grade or that broken arm in high school or a broken heart in college or the broken marriage.

But you can choose to learn from these teachers.

Back to school? You bet.

Today, every day, until the last breath.

Here's to a happy, healthier New Year!

Truth and Freedom

When I was living and working in East Harlem (NYC), I met many people who went to "the rooms", their way of describing the places that held Alcoholics Anonymous meetings. To understand what people were going through during their struggles with sobriety I picked up expressions that I soon found were also helpful outside "the rooms."

Here are just a few:

- A.A. is a self-help program that you can't do by yourself.
- Sometimes what happens is that "hurt people hurt people."
- You'll only stop abusing alcohol when you're "sick and tired of being sick and tired."
- The destiny of every alcoholic is to be "locked up, covered up or sobered up."
- It (the program) works if you work it.
- One drink is too many and a thousand isn't enough.

One phrase that is eminently applicable to any life is: "I am as sick as my secrets." As a Life Coach (or *Behavior Redesigner*), I know how freeing it is for people to live honest, open lives:

I read somewhere years ago that if you never tell a lie you don't have to have a good memory.

What truths might you sometimes hide behind and why? If you would like to unburden your heart or merely share an issue that's holding you back, find someone (such as a Life Coach) and ask them to work with you.

On a lighter note, recovering alcoholics were some of the finest people I met (and still know). Many of them have amazing outlooks on life given the calamities they had caused. They are also some of the funniest folks around. Here's a sample of their humor:

> Me: My name is Matt, and I'm an alcoholic.
> AAA: This is AAA, not AA.
> Me: Yeah, I was just explaining how my car got in the lake.

> What do you call an alcoholic that doesn't admit his addiction?
> Jack Denials.

> Why can't alcoholics become lawyers?
> They can't pass the bar.

> I come from a long line of alcoholics. My gene pool has a swim-up bar.

> Alcoholics don't run in my family?
> They stumble around and break stuff.

> Why didn't the alcoholic become a comedian?
> Because he couldn't stand up.

Daniel Francis

Get S.M.A.R.T. in 2021

Happy New Year! Wow. We made it! I'm betraying my age with the title of this reflection- how many of you remember the mostly black and white series from the late 60s (starring Don Adams and Barbara Feldon): Get Smart?

There is a business phrase that goes "work smarter not harder." That's my hope for you as you begin this new year.

In 1981 George T. Doran submitted a theory for writing goals and objectives. He utilized a mnemonic acronym called "SMART":

> Specific – target a specific area for improvement
> Measurable – quantify an indicator of progress
> Assignable – specify who, if anybody, am I waiting for to get it done
> Realistic – state what results can realistically be achieved
> Time-related – specify when the result(s) can be achieved

What would SMART living look like for you?

Physically, it could be weight loss, exercise, eating healthier or getting more sleep

Spiritually, you might begin to meditate daily, get back to worship or pick up an inspirational book

Mentally, consider mindfulness practice to help you create a cleaner space in your mind and heart

Emotionally, the first step might mean forgiving yourself, someone else, or a person (perhaps deceased) who may have hurt you

<u>Interpersonally</u>, do you need to connect with real people, honest people or maybe disconnect from those who bring you down?

Why wait... do it today!

As the memorable line goes in the movie, The Best Exotic Marigold Hotel: "It will be alright in the end and if it's not all right it's not the end."

Daniel Francis

Lagom

On the wall just outside our family kitchen when I was
growing up, Mom hung a golden frieze of Jesus and his
disciples. Having purchased it in Spain--my father was
stationed there as a Navy decoder-- the inscription read:
"La Ultima Cena de Jesus" (Jesus' Last Supper). I was
fascinated by the fact that I could decode the words from
another language.

Years later, learning French and Latin only fueled my
curiosity surrounding etymology, linguistics and philology.
For example, did you know that the word muscle comes
from Latin (*musculus*) meaning "little mouse" because
people believed that the movement of tendons looked like
mice running underneath the skin?

Or that salary, also from Latin is derived from "salt
money" (*salarium*) and, due to its importance, was valued as
"white gold." For instance, it was used to treat wounds
(thus the word salutary--or healthy--comes from salt). In
old times, laborers were paid with salt that they could use
to preserve their food.

All this to share a new word I learned: *lagom* (noun);
origin: Swedish, early 19th century:

> "The principle of living a balanced, moderately
> paced, low-fuss life."

Norwegians also use the word, lagom, to talk about living
"just about right": the right amount, the right time, the
right approach. How refreshing is this concept. It's so....
right!

May I remind you that "rightness" is more than a feeling-
you know, those fleeting emotions that derive from
neurochemicals in the brain which are notoriously

superficial and fickle.

Living a right life is being at peace with this moment in front of me- whatever it is. Someone sitting at a dinner table on the night before his murder surrounded by a traitor and 11 friends drew from this peace.

We can, too.

Daniel Francis

An Inside Job

We are now into day five of this new year. With the
promise of COVID-19 vaccination (we know a few people
who have received their first "jab") and increased
production and shipment, hope is in the air.

There's a house for sale in our neighborhood. Out front is
the usual sign with the realtor's name, number and agency.
But underneath the sign is an alluring message inviting
people to take a look around, boasting: "I'm beautiful
inside." How many of us believe that?

I can assure you that if you live knowing yourself to be
beautiful and worthy of love, you probably have less stress
than most, need fewer pills and take more risks. If you
operate from a deep certainty that you are lovely inside and
out, chances are you don't worry about what others think,
cannot bruise easily and find it easy to accept others'
imperfections.

The new year is still young and this week has just begun.
If you've made some resolutions but have slipped, start
again after asking yourself what happened? If you haven't
articulated any goals yet, consider this (from a weekly blog
I read) as you write them:

> What you say matters less than what you do.
> New goals won't get you different results.
> Different actions can.
> Change what you're doing to change where you're
> going.

If you want to see what really matters to you, look at how
you spend your time.

Let's make these years the Roaring '20s. Not wild or
unruly but filled with joy and expectancy and gratitude.

Disease, disaster, dissension or disagreements will not define us. We are made for more than these- higher and brighter.

If a house for sale can proclaim itself to be beautiful, what is stopping you?

Alternatively, near the gas station is a placard that says "I buy ugly houses." Hey, beauty is in the eye of the re-builder.

Daniel Francis

Capitol Oneness

On Wednesday afternoon of this week I was on the phone
with a friend when his wife interrupted the call to say that
protestors had just breached the United States capitol
building. After hanging up, I turned on the television to
find out what was happening. It reminded me of 9/11.
Even though personally I was not a building terrorized nor
a victim of any physical harm, I felt a visceral violation in
my body.

Where does one go in the midst of such brutality without
and discord within? I think of don Miguel Ruiz's 5 guides
to personal freedom:

1. Be impeccable with your word
2. Don't take anything personally
3. Don't make assumptions
4. Always do your best
5. Be skeptical, but learn to listen

I heard a story years ago of a therapist who came home
each night exhausted by all the tragic and stressful stories
she heard and helped navigate through with her clients.

She came up with the idea to touch a tree's bark before she
entered the house and "leave all her negativity outside"
where it could possibly be used to "fertilize" the tree; this
reminded me of all the banana peels, coffee grounds and
eggshells that composted for our family home's shrubbery
mulch.

If you've been reading enough of my reflections, then you
understand the inference I'm making. Whatever response
(or reaction!) you have to what's going on in the District of
Columbia these days, pay attention to your own district-
that place that is mostly in your control.

Be careful of what you say aloud (see guide #1 above);
avoid internalizing (guide #2); filter a lot of the news
(guide #3); let this mess inspire the best in you (guide #4);
and (guide #5) listen for the hurts in other people, the
"other side", our nation and world.

No one loses what can't be stolen.

Written in one of the corridors in our nation's Capitol is
this quote from Daniel Webster: "One country, one
Constitution, one destiny."

Daniel Francis

Time and Tempo

"It is easy to be bleak about the human race, but there are people who have proved to me that we can be better than we are," writes Dr. Peniel Joseph.

After the events of last week, I continue to look for and draw inspiration from people who remind us of our best and highest. Proofs of human goodness are everywhere and always outnumber instances of cruelty and hatred.

How is it possible we are 12 days into the new year? How relative time is. I've heard parents of young children say that sometimes one minute lasts an hour and a year is like a day. The author of a memoir I recently finished agrees:

> "The days are long but the years are short," some say about the early years of child rearing. I remember some days being almost gelid in their slowness when Solo was a baby. I had never experienced time so consciously.
>
> Collapsed on the bed with him in strong afternoon sunshine, holding him up to the light and watching the light inside of him, listening to his birdsong. Time moved as though through honey.
> -Elizabeth Alexander, *The Light of the World: A Memoir*

The year is still so young with all sorts of possibilities. It's almost like a blank slate. We have the ability to re-start (or course correct) at any time, any day or even this hour.

There's something very rich and perfect about a January RESET. And there is no time like the present to do this.

How about some possibilities?

Reading this, understand that YOU set the tempo for your

life. Why? Because you probably know better than anyone when things are right with you, as well as when something is amiss. Don't let anyone rush you, but be careful not to allow inertia to sabotage your energy output.

Supporting and Defending

If the word "augur" means to portend, no one pretends
that tomorrow's inauguration will fix everything. Similar
to four years ago, nearly half of voting Americans will be
glad and others will be sad. And yet we move on. The key
is that we move.

Or, as T. S. Eliot put it in The Four Quartets: "to be still
and still moving."

What is true is that no matter who is president, we are the
commander-in-chief of our individual lives. We can play
the blame game, get upset with circumstances outside of us
(and outside of our control) or we can take our own oath
of home (or office, if you prefer):

> As I begin this new year, this new term of my life,
> I do solemnly affirm that I will support and
> defend all that I hold dear in the state of my
> united body and mind and soul:
>> -against the enemies of negativity, self-
>> doubt, excuse-making
>> -both foreign (others' moods, opinions
>> and outer circumstances)
>> -and domestic (inner struggles with the
>> deepest truth of myself)
>> -without any purpose of evasion but
>> rather right intentionality and clear
>> choice-making
> And I will faithfully discharge the duties and
> delights of this one life I have been given, so help
> me God.

Cue the roaring crowd, applause and affirmation. So
begins your term. I can't wait to hear your State of the Self
next year at this time!

Growing Stronger at Broken Places
[4 thoughts]

Thought #1: Years ago when I was watching a football game, I heard the announcers comment about an injured player saying that a fracture is better than a dislocation; it heals faster.

Thought #2: In his book, *The Broken Among Us Teach Us*, Bryan Stevenson writes that "it's really the broken among us that know something about what it means to be human... something about grace... It's the broken among us that can teach us some things. And knowing that you don't have to be perfect and complete gives you a way of dealing with what looks impossible."

Thought #3: Aldous Huxley wrote: "It's dark because you are trying too hard. Lightly child, lightly. Learn to do everything lightly. Yes, feel lightly even though you're feeling deeply. Just lightly let things happen and lightly cope with them."

Final thought: As our nation continues to heal from COVID, Political Rancor, Racism, Blaming, Economic Stress and many other maladies, may we--in the midst of all the brokenness--celebrate and respect our differences while honoring our strength as one nation under God, indivisible with liberty and justice for all.

N.B.: The title for this reflection comes from a book by the same name.

Live Long(er) and Prosper

Generally, optimists live longer. You might quickly come up with an exception to that rule. But in a 2020 longevity research, optimists or people who expect "that good things will happen, believing that the future will be favorable because they can control important outcomes" not only live more years but enjoy healthier years.

I resonate with this notion that people can set goals and control important aspects of their own future.

You see, optimism is highly related to having a sense of agency and purpose.

Purpose has already been shown in many studies to be a prime factor in elders' happiness as they age. It also lowers the risk of premature death, promotes healthy behaviors and friendships, and staves off loneliness.

So, if you feel unhealthy or alone, what can you do?

First of all, it's important to understand and embrace the truth that you don't have to be this way. Unless you are dealing with deep, irrational and/or psychological issues that need to be treated by a therapist, your thinking is just that: merely your thinking. Unlike the weather or your neighbor's mood, you can change your thinking. This is not just a nice sentiment bandied about by New Age hawkers; I truly believe that if you "change your thinking, you change your life!"

As you believe in the possibility of your own soul, believe it is God.

As you believe in God, believe in yourself. The more you believe in yourself, the greater becomes your love for others (of any stripe) and your optimism in a better world, co-created by your actions, is happening before you.

Do this and you will live happily and eventually die in peace, joy and great hope that you are leaving a better world than the one into which you were born.

Daniel Francis

R.E.S.P.E.C.T.

There is a running debate about the word "tolerance." To some, it means accepting others for what they believe, how they behave and the ideas they behold, even if you don't agree.

To others, tolerance is akin to begrudgingly allowing something I don't care for. One is based on respect; the other comes from judgment.

An emperor named Ashoka, who ruled India in the third century before Christ, declared in an edict which can still be seen inscribed on pillars near Delhi, "Anybody who is disrespectful of other religions has no respect for his own."

Whatever your political "color" or your views about everything from the climate to vaccines to the economy and beyond... my wish is that we have a more respectful tolerance for those with whom we don't agree.

February Forward

We are a month into the new year. How are you doing
with your resolutions? Over 87% of us make them.
Unfortunately, research shows that 45% of people fail to
keep their resolutions by February, and only 19% keep
them for two years.

Lack of willpower or self-control is the top-cited reason
for not following through.

The good news is: YOU CAN START AGAIN. Just
make today the beginning of your "new year", so to speak.

Below are 7 suggestions (adapted from various sources) to
help you:

1. Honestly ask yourself why you want to do (or not do)
something. Whether your new resolution is to lose weight,
exercise, meditate or avoid sugar, ask Why? What is
driving you to achieve this goal? When you're clear about
your values, your energy matches the drive needed.

2. Articulate your goal(s) in a positive way. Instead of
saying, "I want to drink less booze," hear yourself saying
"I am going to enjoy more tea or sparkling water in the
evenings." Be grateful that you have the options you have;
leave negativity behind. You are doing this for a healthier,
happier you. There is nothing negative about that.

3. Have your family/spouse/friend/co-worker/life coach
be your accountability partner. Allow them to remind you
of the goal(s) you have shared with them and that you are
serious about working on. Empower them with the ability
to call you on weakness or excuses. If your partner is
inappropriate or invasive, choose someone else. This
could be very fun AND you might end up helping to keep
them accountable one day as a favor exchanged.

4. Out of sight, (kinda) out of mind. Remove the pop-tarts or credit cards. Keep no visual reminders of what you want to avoid. But remember to... (#5)

5. Place notecards/PostIts with positive messages where you can see them. Move a scale near the closet (along with a progress sheet and pen). Keep your walking/running shoes in a conspicuous place. Have Alexa or Siri set a daily timer to remind you.

6. Know your triggers ahead of time and think out your actions. For example, if it's Friday night and you don't feel like cooking but the store has a pizza that will microwave in 30 minutes, what are you going to buy instead? It's Saturday morning and cold outside, what is stopping you from bundling up for your jog? Envision your weakest moments as well as the joy of vanquishing them and you will feel the energy of your positivity winning out in the end. If not...

7. Be compassionate with yourself if you have a setback. A study shows that people who harshly blame themselves for even small willpower failures tend to do worse in accomplishing their goals in the long run. So, if you gorge on M&Ms, relax. Ask yourself what this is filling in you (besides your stomach)? If you don't write your book for 30 minutes that day, find out why and then recommit yourself to the goal. Start again tomorrow.

Need any help articulating goals and/or working on accountability? That's what I do!

Ordinary Miracles

Albert Einstein is often quoted as saying that "there are only two ways to live your life: as if nothing is a miracle and as if everything is a miracle."

I'm sure there is plenty of middle ground between cynicism and mysticism, but if you tend toward one end or the other, it probably characterizes the way you view life.

Richard Rohr is fond of saying "How you do your NOW is how you do your life."

Life is chock full of what looks ordinary. Consider these instances:

- As I stand waiting for the always hot water to pass through a cup of coffee grounds into a K-cup, I look at our kitchen window bird feeder and see two finches deftly cracking open safflower seeds to reveal the edible portion. Ordinary.
- A nurse works a 12-hour shift, comes home, thanks the masked babysitter, feeds and bathes the kids, reads a bedtime story, watches the news, falls asleep and it's time for work again. Ordinary.
- On our nightly walk, we watch the moon's halo increase with breathtaking color. Ordinary.
- A teacher spends one day driving by her students' homes with a honk of the horn and a sign that says, "I'm so proud of you." Ordinary.
- A bald eagle flies from a neighbor's pine tree across the lake and out of sight. Ordinary.
- Two old friends reunite... online. Neither has used Zoom before nor cried as much in many years. Ordinary.

Extraordinary.

Daniel Francis

As they say, it is the little "extra" that makes it so!

Read these words to a beautiful song called "Ordinary Miracles":

Change can come on tiptoe
Love is where it starts
It resides, often hides
Deep within our hearts
And just as
Pebbles make a mountain,
Raindrops make a sea,
One day at a time
Change begins with you and me,
Ordinary miracles
Happen all around,
Just by giving and receiving
Comes belonging and believing,
Every sun that rises
Never rose before,
Each new day leads the way
Through a different door,
And we can all be quiet heroes
Living quiet days,
Walking through the world
Changing it in quiet ways,
Ordinary miracles
Like candles in the dark,
Each and every one of us
Lights a spark,
And the walls can tumble
And the mountains can move,
The winds and the tide can turn,
Yes, ordinary miracles
One for every star,
No lightning bolt or clap or thunder
Only joy and quiet wonder,
Endless possibilities

Right before our eyes,
Oh, see the way a miracle multiples,
Now hope can spring eternally
Plant it and it grows,
Love is all that's necessary
Lovin', its extraordinary way
Makes ordinary miracles every blessed day.

Thank God It's Friday

When I was in middle school, on the cusp of a holiday or perhaps just because it was Friday, as the clock's minute hand inched its way to 3:00 PM, some brave soul would start chanting "No more pencils, no more books, no more teachers' dirty looks; when the teacher rings the bell, drop your books and run like hell." [Quick apologies to several teachers who read these reflections.]

The same is true in the work world- you see (or remember in pre-COVID times) images of the industrial complex's whistle at full 5:00 throttle, employees time-carding out, the snarl of rush hour traffic, the promise to stop at the bar for a brewsky... it's Friday!

Funny, I was going to caption this reflection: That Sunday Nite Feeling

Sunday is, obviously, the opposite and tail end of the weekend, but it's also the "last gasp" before the mundane of the workweek. But if you want to shed the unsettling feeling on a Sunday evening that the weekend has gone by too swiftly, there is something you can do: pause as often as you can, look around, appreciate what you have, who you have it with (if you do), your relative health with which to enjoy it and be grateful.

Youth is not wasted on the young as long as we can enjoy the time we have as we can. I'll let the words of someone else end today's reflection. I believe if you read it slowly, you can hear and feel the grace of time that we are given.

> It's Friday! The way we experience time in our minds is never going to match up with the latest discoveries in physics. We all know what the passing of time feels like. Although we can't change the way our brains perceive time, there are

better ways we can start to think about it. But even then, the way it warps in certain situations will continue to surprise and unsettle us. In the end, perhaps, St Augustine put it best when he asked: "What then is time? If no one asks me, then I know. If I wish to explain it to someone who asks, I know it not."

Claudia Hammond,
Time Warped: Unlocking The Secrets Of Time Perception.

Mind Opening

Over this past year, the concept of certainty has become... well, uncertain.

The CDC initially tells us one thing and then it gets changed. Anyone with a large digital megaphone says something and, unchecked, it becomes fact and creates a polarizing line-in-the-sand to those on the "other side."

Perhaps we ourselves make proclamations about how we are doing which get summarily upended. Security seems fragile and handrails untrustworthy. Teachers are supposed to be everywhere, right? But who guides us to interpret the litmus test for veracity?

Adam Grant writes in *Think Again* that in a tempestuous world, intelligence might not be as important as the ability to rethink and unlearn. He says: "Mental horsepower doesn't guarantee mental dexterity."

No matter how much brainpower you have, if you lack the motivation to change your mind, you'll miss many occasions to think again.

Research reveals that the higher you score on an IQ test, the more likely you are to fall for ste-reotypes, because you're faster at recognizing patterns.

And recent experiments suggest that the smarter you are, the more you might struggle to update your beliefs.

The curse of confidence is that it can close your mind to what you don't know. On the other hand, the wise person keeps his/her mind open.

I'm not saying this isn't scary, but just as a child eventually unlearns Santa Claus and the Easter Bunny, could it be that one of the many lessons of this pandemic is to know when it's time to let go of some of the most cherished--but old, non-functioning and perhaps destructive--parts of our identity and belief system?

Daniel Francis

"How's That?"

It's growing weaker, but I still have a very keen sense of hearing. When I was a northerner, I could hear snow falling on the evergreen branches outside the window; often I hear the sprinklers come on in the early morning or the call of the limpkin from a mile away near the lake. On a side note, ask Alice and she'll tell you sometimes I can't hear her from the next room! Have you ever noticed how deafening is the silence once the fridge motor turns off; you get so accustomed to hearing the background noise that the lack of sound is at once a surprise and a relief.

There are moments during our afternoon walks when there are no words between my wife and me- simply the peace of the present as we gaze at familiar sights that consistently inspire new appreciation.

So it is when taking time to meditate or at least consciously pausing for mindfulness. There is nothing to do: nothing to clean or fold or scrub or write or post or judge or worry about or prepare for or study or ignore or remember...

There is literally nothing--NO THING--to do or be or become or oppose.

I find it fascinating that the word "listen" is found in "silent" when you scramble the letters. If you try it, you'll like it.

Noticing Things

There's a scene in the musical "Music Man" whereby
Marian (Shirley Jones) realizes she's in love with Professor
Harold Hill (Robert Preston) and sings:

> There were bells on the hill
> But I never heard them ringing
> No, I never heard them at all
> Till There Was You...

I've heard and read how some people speak of liminal
moments in their life when they became awake, aware,
alive. In a drama series that we are watching, the main
character--after being diagnosed with stage 4 cancer--
exclaims" "I feel woke!"

Might I suggest that one of the silver linings during these
troubling pandemic times might be that people have been
forced to slow down and re-think goals, values and
priorities. Even as we have exceeded that sad, sobering
number of 500,000 American COVID-19 deaths, perhaps
the disease can be the catalyst for more focused energy.

As an example, the other day a friend of ours turned 92.
Despite the virus, Sal has not slowed down a bit, is careful
to protect his and others' health and yet has still managed
to write, publish and narrate a book.

What I know to be true is that the more you listen and
learn, without first judging and labeling, the wider your
acceptance becomes for diversity.

As my mom would say to us kids, "How boring would life
be if everyone were the same." And guess what? When
you are open to learning, you "kick it up a notch", as chef
Emeril would say. Concentrating and noticing even the
little things inspires neurogenesis (the birth of new brain

cells) which works to improve your cognitive reserve, your mind's resiliency, and makes you less likely to develop dementia.

Finally, as George Washington Carver once wrote: "I love to think of nature as unlimited broadcasting stations, through which God speaks to us every day, every hour."

May something you notice today inspire in you a most astonishing sense of aliveness!

Wandering Mind- part 1

I blame and bless Crocket Johnson's book, *Harold and the Purple Crayon* for distractions and delights. The story involves the title character who wants to go for a walk at night, but as there is no moon, he draws one. Then, with nowhere to walk, little Harold sketches a path. You get the concept. My 5th-grade mind whirred with the idea that I, too, could have the power to create a world of my own simply by drawing it.

Letting your mind wander, Sandi Mann, a British psychologist, has said, "makes us more creative, better at problem-solving, better at coming up with creative ideas." The Dutch have a word for this concept: *niksen*, or the art of doing nothing.

Pascal once said, "All of humanity's difficulties are caused by the inability to sit quietly in a room by oneself." In a world of non-stop notifications, alerts, beeps and buzzes; where the TV or radio has to be on; in which multi-tasking threatens to simultaneously rob us of energy and get less done... perhaps we need to schedule time to do nothing.

Recently a woman in an online chat group I sometimes contribute to posted this:

> Meditation is my go-to, especially when compulsivity gets the best of me. At some point, given enough alone time, and the quiet of meditation, forces the admission that if I still feel so miserable in the midst of being so alone, I might also be the source of those feelings. This leads to the miraculous insight that given enough quiet time, my feelings will, and do, settle down.

As Amos Tversky, a pathbreaking psychologist, said, "You

waste years by not being able to waste hours."

If you are wondering why your mind wanders, perhaps you can intentionally wander in your mind and stop worrying.

H.A.L.T.

When I was maybe 7 or 8, something got me upset. In a household of nine, it could have been any number of possibilities: an older sister had eaten my potato chips or an older brother didn't ask to borrow my toy or my only younger sibling might have looked at me the wrong way.

I don't remember why I was so upset; I do recall how I calmed down.

Or rather, how I was forced to calm down.

My oldest brother, Tony, probably tired of the noise and spectacle of my tantrum, decided to help me. Holding me in a tight hug, he instructed me that he would not let go until I counted to ten.

It took a few attempts, but eventually it worked: he quite literally hugged the anger out of me.

In my training, I learned about the acronym H.A.L.T. which stands for Hungry, Angry, Lonely or Tired.

The idea is that when you are experiencing one or more of these emotions, STOP. Don't lash out. Don't post. Don't send that email. Don't speak!

Find out where the feelings are coming from and put some distance between them and your mind.

Daniel Francis

Growing Old(er)

Do you remember the first time you were not asked to show an ID? Did someone ever ask you prematurely if you wanted the AARP or Senior Citizen price? Some people get hit hard the day they realize they're getting older. Others, like my friend Tom, boast about all the perks, discounts and freebies they begin to get. I would say that what bothers folks is more about vanity than mortality.

You see, beginning to look older impacts people in different ways, often prompting a "fight or flight" reaction: in the extreme, that might mean plastic surgery, a new hair color or buying a gym membership to get in better shape.

On the other hand, the person may deny all the changes are happening and might even withdraw from social activities or manifest symptoms of depression.

The good news is that you can beat the graying blues by realizing your meaning and purpose. It might sting or inspire but getting older definitely causes us to question both the path that we've followed as well as the path ahead. The power of thinking about this becomes an important inflection point from who we've been to who we aim to become.

Truthfully, there does not need to be a midlife crisis; growing older can be thought of as an opportunity. The Japanese have a highly energetic attitude on aging that goes like this: Discover the happiness derived from devoting your time to an activity that holds meaning and purpose for you.

Because meaning and purpose, combined with calm and healthy living, will mostly likely lead you to a fulfilling and long life.

There's no denying the fact that the past twelve months have been a challenge for many, maybe even a burden for some. My wife and I often say that we are not <u>reality deniers</u>; it's just that we choose to see the possibilities amid the pain and problems. Solutions are more satisfying than blaming and sulking.

So, what are you going to do with the "rest of your life?" As Vivian Diller, Ph.D. writes, "It used to be, 'I have so little time left.' Now it's 'I have so much time left. Do I want to live life this way?'" Our hope at Alive 'n Well is that you are on your way to the answer. And we're not too proud to hope that we are helping you get there!

Daniel Francis

Wondering Mind- part 2

In a previous reflection, I referenced one of my favorite childhood storybooks about a boy with a magical crayon that allows him to create a world of his choosing.

Imagine if that were true. Seriously. With your mind, you could create a new life for yourself. What would it be like? Would you have better health, more money, closer friends, a safer world, no climate crisis, racial/gender respect and equality?

Now picture it's the following day. You awaken. You didn't sleep well (maybe it was the bed or something you ate). Okay, you slept well but the coffee is out. Okay, you have your coffee and you look at emails and there are too many. Okay, they are manageable, but your computer is slow and taking forever to load a message from your bank. Okay, that's all fine but your neighbor's dog is loose on your lawn or it's raining and you had wanted to get in a powerwalk or the news just mentioned a politician whom you despise..... you get the idea, right?

This is not meant to be a bummer reflection. It's my attempt to circle back to your magical crayon. You have the power to create the world of your choice... internally! Of course, there are ways you can contribute to (make better or bitter) the universe that exists outside of you: you can be pleasant or impatient; you can be peace-seeking online or antagonistic.

But, as Sanja Gupta writes in a book I'm reading (*Keep Sharp: Build a Better Brain at Any Age*), referring to a traumatic time in his family's life when his father had been mugged and he himself felt as if the culprit had taken something from him... he spoke to a teacher about it who told him, "They can take away everything you own, but they can never take away this" (pointing to his head).

Who's controlling how you feel? Do you easily give away your peace to the person who bothers you? What life could you have right now if you drew it up in your mind without depending on outside circumstances or conditions?

That's your true life. Live it.

Daniel Francis

Getting Bold(er)

There are, among others, two ways of aging: gruffly or gracefully. We've all witnessed the disturbed or distracted older person who is just not themselves. Something just isn't cooperating inside of them. On the other hand, there is the unmistakable beauty of someone who lives boldly without being a bother.

At some point, you begin to realize that our life is all one integrated whole- each component enhancing the others to equal something greater than the sum of its parts.

And there's one crucial organ where that integration comes together in the most evident fashion: your brain.

- Exercise and nutrition enhance your brain.
- Continuing to do challenging work enhances your brain.
- Personal projects such as reading and learning enhance your brain.

While there's nothing to fear about getting older (remember, age is truly just a number), cognitive decline or dementia frightens most everyone, especially those who are advancing in years.

My father had Alzheimer's and perhaps that's made me very aware of good brain health.

In a recent interview, Dr. Sanjay Gupta offered that putting your brain health first is the essence of integrated well-being: everything else is derivative from that.

You're much more likely to improve all other aspects of your health if you start with your brain health.

If for no other reason, you'll have better judgment.

You'll make better decisions about the other things in your life that affect your health, such as how you nourish your body.

In other words, we can start settling into predictable routines and old beliefs that lead to our mental decline as we age.

Or, we can actively look for new experiences and challenges now that will become an integral part of who we are becoming. Dr. Gupta argues that you've got to get outside your current comfort zone: take on new projects that challenge you in a way that's almost a bit scary; adopt a regimen of diet and exercise that is good for your heart and your head at the same time.

I've written before in these reflections about neurogenesis. It's basically the concept of birthing new brain cells.

There is enough supportive science to prove that learning and reading and trying new things essentially create new pathways in your brain that keep you sharp.

On the other hand, if you settle into the predictable, repetitive routines you've followed for years, your neurological roads start to narrow.

I can't place the source but I read somewhere that not only do your reasoning skills weaken, but your ability to empathize also gets "blocked" because your brain cells won't make the appropriate connections.

That's why some elderly say outrageous things. They are not being bold so much as suffering from an ability to understand what is going on in that situation. We may laugh at their outspokenness when really it's a sign of incremental cognitive decline.

Daniel Francis

Whatever your conception of "your best life" is, it's rightly all in your head.

The three-pound organ in your skull is the primary key to living the life you want.

That's something to keep in mind when you don't feel like pushing yourself for better health, wealth, and personal growth.

Grow older and be smarter, healthier and bolder about the way you're using your brain. You've got this!

"Ashes, Ashes"

For Christians around the world, today is the beginning of Lent marked by Ash Wednesday. Some people are inspired to give up beer or butterscotch in order to self-impose a holy discipline to greet Easter with a stronger heart and healthier soul.

My classmate, Father Byron Miller, is president of a leading national Catholic magazine called *Liguorian*. In a recent issue, he included a piece by Carole St. Laurent on the need to re-envision LOVE as "the key ingredient that our global family needs now more than ever."

She concludes the article by creatively paraphrasing the words of the Apostle Paul when he wrote to the community at Corinth:

> If I get more retweets and likes than anyone, but my words lack love, it would be better if I never posted.
> If I can predict the pandemic curve, sell millions of masks, and even create the best vaccine, but profit from others' pain instead of prevent it, my net worth is the inverse of my human worth.
>
> If I have enough faith to heal hundreds of COVID-19 patients, but am unmoved by love for them, I am nothing.
>
> Love is everything.
>
> Love is patient, love is kind, even when it has to stand in line.
>
> Love is not jealous of those with the all-clear; it perseveres and self-quarantines until there's no virus to fear.

Love is not too proud to put on a mask; it would rather protect one vulnerable person than demand convenience for itself.

Love is not rude, its gentle answers calm down wrath; it soothes the souls of those whose nerves are just about shot.

Love doesn't hold grudges, rather it's quick to forgive; for those who love the most are the most aware of their own sin.

Love resists the temptation to forward fake news; it checks rumors, deletes insults, and only shares life-affirming truths.

When love is weary, it rests in Jesus' strength; there it finds the faith, hope, and love to carry on, finding love the most strong.

My child, love on.

Lens Cleaning

In one of my favorite movies of the '80s, *Aliens*, the monsters are bearing down on two soldiers. One of them blurts out, "This ain't happening, man!"

His response reminds me of the scared child who hopes that closing her eyes will change what she fears.

On this theme, Richard Rohr writes:

> People with a distorted image of self, world, or God will be largely incapable of experiencing what is really real in the world. They will see things through a narrow keyhole. They'll see instead what they need reality to be, what they're afraid it is, or what they're angry about. They'll see everything through their aggressiveness, their fear, or their agenda. In other words, they won't see it at all.

From my own inner work, I struggle with seeing things as they are. But what I've come to understand is that strong, mature people see reality as it is, whether favorable or not, whether it suits them or not, whether what is seen brings joy or tears. Most of us, however, have too much of the ego in the way and either fight with reality or try to tame it through naming and judging.

We need support in unmasking our false self and in distancing ourselves from our illusions.

In a webinar I gave last year, I spoke about how it's helpful to install a kind of "inner observer" or what some call a "fair witness."

When you catch yourself (over)reacting to something you have seen on TV, online, or on social media, turn off your inner namer and inner judger and watch yourself. Then

Daniel Francis

ask a series of questions: Do I need to merge my emotions
with what I'm seeing? Can I merely notice what I'm feeling
and then let that go?

What would change in me if I could read or hear without
having my emotions kidnapped?

Impermanence

The tabebuia is a tree that grows almost everywhere in our neighborhood. During this time of the year, when the leaves of oaks and elms, maples and willows are popping with nearly every hue of green imaginable, when the bougainvilleas, azaleas and irises seem to be vying for attention, I think of the first and last lines of a poem by Robert Frost: "Nature's first green is gold/Her hardest hue to hold...for nothing gold can stay."

I recently read that in 1859, before he was president, before he suffered through that harrowing train ride to Washington on his way to office where many thought he would be killed before he arrived, before the Union tore itself to pieces and around 750,000 people died in the Civil War, Abraham Lincoln gave a speech at the Wisconsin State Fair.

The topic of the speech was supposed to be agriculture, but Lincoln decided to go a little deeper.

He told the story of a king who asked his wisest philosophers to provide for him a sentence that would be not just true in each and every situation, but always worth hearing.

> "They presented him the words," Lincoln said, "'And this, too, shall pass away.'" How much it expresses! How chastening in the hour of pride!—how consoling in the depths of affliction! 'And this, too, shall pass away.'"

Did Lincoln know that he had less than six years left to live, with which to do his work, before he too would pass away?

I have to tell you that the meaning behind this reflection is

Daniel Francis

not to "grab the gold" before it goes, but to know that this moment can never be grabbed, bottled nor chained down.

But how GRATEFUL I am for memories and pictures.

Good Rules- Two Sets

Some years ago, after my parents moved from Maryland to Florida to begin the second half of their life, they bought a print of H. Jackson Brown's *Life's Little Instructions*. If you've never read them, they are:

Sing in the shower. Treat everyone you meet like you want to be treated. Watch a sunrise at least once a year. Never refuse homemade brownies. Strive for excellence, not perfection. Plant a tree on your birthday. Learn three clean jokes. Return borrowed vehicles with the gas tank full. Compliment three people every day. Never waste an opportunity to tell someone you love them. Keep it simple. Think big thoughts but relish small pleasures. Become the most positive and enthusiastic person you know. Floss your teeth. Ask for a raise when you feel you've earned it. Be forgiving of yourself and others. Overtip breakfast waitresses. Say "thank you" a lot. Say "please" a lot. Avoid negative people. Buy whatever kids are selling on card tables in their front yards. Wear polished shoes. Remember other people's birthdays. Commit yourself to constant improvement. Carry jumper cables in your trunk. Have a firm handshake. Send lots of Valentine cards. Look people in the eye. Be the first to say "Hello". Use the good silver. Return all things you borrow. Make new friends but cherish the old ones. Keep secrets. Sing in a choir. Plant flowers every spring. Have a dog. Always accept an outstretched hand. Stop blaming others. Take responsibility for every area of your life. Wave at kids on school buses. Be there when people need you. Feed a stranger's expired parking meter. Don't expect life to be fair. Never underestimate the power of love. Drink champagne for no reason at all. Live your life as an exclamation, not an explanation. Don't be afraid to say "I made a mistake". Don't be afraid to say "I don't know". Compliment even small improvements. Keep your

Daniel Francis

promises (no matter what). Marry only for love. Rekindle
old friendships. Count your blessings. Call your mother.

And in 2016, the songwriter Lori McKenna crafted a tune
that was written for her five young children and that has
since become a hit for Tim McGraw. She puts together a
really heartfelt list of "rules", and captures it all well in the
chorus.

> Visit grandpa every chance that you can
> It won't be a waste of time
> Always stay humble and kind
> Hold the door say please say thank you
> Don't steal, don't cheat, and don't lie
> I know you got mountains to climb but
> Always stay humble and kind
> When the dreams you're dreamin' come to you
> When the work you put in is realized
> Let yourself feel the pride but
> Always stay humble and kind

> Don't expect a free ride from no one
> Don't hold a grudge or a chip and here's why
> Bitterness keeps you from flying
> Always stay humble and kind
> Know the difference between sleeping with someone
> And sleeping with someone you love
> I love you ain't no pick up line so
> Always stay humble and kind
> Don't take for granted the love this life gives you
> When you get where you're goin'
> Don't forget turn back around
> Help the next one in line
> Always stay humble and kind

The Way We View Reality

It's now been more than a year since the pandemic hit Florida with officials urging us to "lockdown/stay-at-home/shelter-in-place", as well as follow the guidelines of masking, distancing and washing.

And this June it will be a year since Alice and I launched this initiative to assist people in terms of health and wellness to be "Alive and Well."

We've learned so much from feedback after our zoominars, through interaction with our posts and as a result of other contact points.

We are grateful for many things but perhaps one in particular rises to the top - and that is the ability to maintain our deep hope and fundamental belief in goodness, beauty and wholeness.

- Goodness: how people give and love and help and inspire one another;
- Beauty: how nature, the earth and sky provide ceaseless awe and wonder; and
- Wholeness: that we are not merely feverish fragments but part of an indivisible unity behind all that is.

Is this too heavy for you? If so, perhaps this woman's words will explain how we feel:

> Often, the person in the group who articulates the possible is dismissed as a dreamer or as a Pollyanna persisting in a simplistic "glass half-full" kind of optimism. The naysayers pride themselves on their supposed realism. However, it is actually the people who see the glass as "half-empty" who are the ones wedded to a fiction, for "emptiness"

Daniel Francis

and "lack" are abstractions of the mind, whereas
"half-full" is a measure of the physical reality
under discussion. The so-called optimist, then, is
the only one attending to real things, the only one
describing a substance that is actually in the glass.

- Rosamund Stone Zander, *The Art of Possibility* (p.
110)

Gotta Grow!

There's an azalea bush in our yard whose curiosity forced it to poke a flower through our fence. I want to think that even the most non-sensate person must find Spring beautiful, if not miraculous.

As a life coach (aka behavior redesigner), I find the beginnings of years and months to be perfect opportunities to try something new or break an old habit.

With Spring officially beginning tomorrow (March 20), why not try something new and different:

- change your online habits (for example, no negative social media posts for a week)
- begin a meditation practice for one month (just five minutes daily is a good start)
- go somewhere to watch the sunset (or peer at it through the window before you settle in for the evening); prepare a different meal this weekend
- turn off the TV and pick up a magazine or book (read something that dazzles or challenges you)
- look to the night sky or find a budding flower

Let Spring inspire you.

Daniel Francis

The Tunnel's End

Yesterday I heard that the CDC warned of a possible "4th Wave" due to a 10% surge in coronavirus cases over the previous week. Gosh, I hope not.

With scenes of spring breakers reveling in Miami Beach and some states actually boasting of being "open for business", it's disappointing. We have worked so hard and endured so many losses: the death of loved ones; canceled graduations, weddings and birthdays; distant pretend hugs and handshakes, empty restaurants and theaters.

Still, the good news is that nearly 70% of people over 65 are fully vaccinated. For our part, we were able to secure our first "jab" two weeks ago.

And, as a recent article in *America* magazine puts it, there are some positive aspects to the pandemic: breaking the code to a novel coronavirus (the previous record for producing a vaccine was 4 years); learning new digital technology (my family zoomed my aunt on Saturday for her 93rd birthday); and a renewed appreciation for our social dynamics (none of us is an island).

Perhaps you, too, can quietly be grateful for something that these past 12+ months have taught you about yourself, your resolve and strength, your ability to "keep on going" and knowing that you are doing what is yours to do.

Not Thick Skin, A Smart Heart

Once in a while, I'll see an interview with a megastar athlete or actor who will confess to being absolutely crushed by what are called "haters", those people who bomb social media or send direct messages with words and emoticons that would probably make a sailor blush.

I suppose that even "back in the day", fan mail included its share of negativity and destructive criticism. But with the ease of speedy posts and texts, the hurt can be hurled even before an actor has removed his makeup or the athlete taken her shower. We all know that it's their choice to be on social media and to read them or not.

What I want to say is that the strong person realizes that being strong does not eliminate all emotion.

It's the regulation of emotion. For example, it's human to be scared or surprised, to be hurt or overjoyed.

What the strong person does, however, is work toward not being ruled by these emotions.

When you feel insulted or bitter, enraged or belittled, DO THE WORK! Find out the origin of these feelings and resist the urge to react.

As Ruth Bader Ginsburg once explained, "My mother's advice was, don't lose time on useless emotions like anger, resentment, remorse, envy. Those, she said, will just sap time; they don't get you where you want to be. One way I coped with times I was angry: I would sit down and practice the piano. I wasn't very good at it, but it did distract me from whatever useless emotion I was feeling at the moment. Later, I did the same with the cello. I would be absorbed in the music, and the useless emotion faded away."

Daniel Francis

We are not automatons without emotion.   When we are at
our best, our knees don't even jerk! We are in control.
Rather than thermometers that only report the
temperature, we are thermostats that change the climate.

We are more than merely a body at the whim of every
feeling originating from the heart and brain.

Showing Your Mettle

I used to find it odd that doctors would order a "stress test" for an individual who was thought to have a potentially weak heart. My thinking: why weaken it or, worse, cause a heart attack. Doctors' thinking: exactly!

As you are probably too well aware that many people do have a cardiac event on that "dread mill" and are admitted right away to ER. Stress tests of aged, yet active bridges and overpasses are different- but the concept is still the same: engineers want to safely reproduce an extreme situation whereby the structure will let them know it needs partial repair or a complete replacement either now or years from now.

Similarly, COVID might be considered a kind of stress test. From already failing businesses to superficial relationships, things that probably needed to "go the way of all good flesh" (as my wry college philosophy professor would call death), just seemed to disappear.

Any outside threat, challenge or obstacle is an opportunity for an individual or a couple. It tests your mettle. It will make you pause and talk; consider action or not; make plans or change course.

But make no mistake: it will make you stronger. I know that's such a cliché but tell me it's not true. Notice I didn't say "it won't make you wince a while or limp a little..." that might happen in the process.

But if it's true that **everything belongs** (the title of a wonderful book by Richard Rohr), then how you confront the toughest thing in front of you right now is illustrative of the strength you bear for the long haul.

Keep training!

Daniel Francis

The Vision Ahead

There's a story told about a very peaceful person who let nothing disturb her. One night, a fire burned away the thatched roof of her humble home. A neighbor who helped put out the fire overheard her say to her husband: "Look, now we can see the moon."

Okay, that might be a little too much for most of us, but one of the lessons is to see what's here instead of what's not.

It's similar to advice given to me by a professor in college. He said that average students are always prepared to recite what is wrong with studies, culture, the nation and life... but the excellent student offers constructive possibilities in the face of challenge. By the time you read this, I will have had my second vaccination. It's my small part in reclaiming the "normal life"- for me, my wife, indeed... and for others.

And as this amazing world comes back alive, opens up again, we can re-imagine.

You have a choice to balk at all that we missed and complain about life interrupted... but the excellent student of life knows that she or he can look beyond what has been to what will be. In a way, it's like a blank slate.

What are you going to create with this new era of your life? Will you go back to the same ways that you didn't care for anyway. Or will you be bold enough to step into a new narrative that says and involves only the best about you: that you care, you love, you matter.

How A Bird and A Nest Reminded Me of Life Lessons

In early April here in Tampa, FL my wife and I saw a pair of cardinals returning often to the thryallis bush just outside our office window. What we expected came to be: they had "nested" about three feet off the ground and our first glimpse of the neatly woven basket—when mother was nowhere near—was of one egg. By the third day, there were three.

These feathered friends remind us of us fundamental lessons:

- loyalty (cardinals mate for life);
- persistence (despite a storm that brought strong winds and 3 inches of rain, the mother cardinal remained at her post);
- patience (she sat for 10 days with few breaks); and of course...
- nurture (when the eggs hatched, she spent nearly all daylight hours foraging for food to drop into gaping beaks).

What instinct commands in animals, humans learn from those who bring us up. If you were raised in a caring, loving, attentive household, you come to appreciate years later the gift of that nourishment.

I'm grateful to my parents for their love and attention... even if I was the sixth child! Despite the fact that potting training me was their sixth time as was wiping away kindergarten tears and looking over multiplication tables and giving driving lessons, their energy was as fresh as it was for the first child.

But I know people whose early life proved wanting in love and compassion. Thankfully they were somehow able to find role models in a surrogate "sister" or "brother" or "parent" when they got older or moved away from home.

In addition to the strength and support of a good home life, I, too, was able to experience another parenting figure in an elderly woman. When I left to enter a high school seminary far from home, I wanted to learn to play the piano.

Mrs. Kohl was a retired music lover who had decided to use her time and energy to develop the talent of new students like me.

I fondly remember how she would place a dime on the top of each of my hands so that I would learn to move only my fingers when practicing scales. Mrs. Kohl also taught me about the great masters of piano composition and played their music for me while enthusiastically describing the "movements" in the pieces.

Although she rarely touched me—perhaps if my posture was stooped or a foot was on the wrong pedal—Mrs. Kohl's presence next to me was somehow metaphysical then and mystical now 40 years later. The nurturing of my young hands and heart with regard to music is something that continues to inspire me to this day.

During this COVID time, amidst the stress and strain of close quarters, monotony, financial worries, suspicious coughs and sudden deaths, we've somehow learned more about one another, even as we sometimes need to get out of the way. We developed new skills and rediscovered old hobbies. No touching allowed, instead we elbow bump or wave on Zoom like school kids looking through bus windows. We have adapted to love and provide empathy through emails, posts and texts.

Eight years after entering the seminary, when I graduated

from college and I had the hutzpah to do so, I asked my mom (half-serious, half-jokingly), "How could you have let me go to a school 600 miles away when I was barely a teen?" Her answer: "Hey, it was one less mouth to feed!" We laughed and then she could tell I really needed to know the answer, so she said, "I trusted you. I knew that if it wasn't right for you, you would have made the correct decision."

As I was finishing this piece, the cardinal chicks became fledglings and then we saw one of them literally "leave the nest" and fly to another part of the same bush. The mother stayed near and fed it for hours. And then both took off. The female cardinal's work is probably done by now. She nurtured her chicks and nature gave us another example of how to do the same with this one, brilliant life and those we love or need to love more.

[This story first appeared at www.insidewink.com.]

Daniel Francis

A Meaningful Life... On Purpose

I have to admit I was thinking the same thing.

During a particularly difficult Math class discussing cotangent, secant and cosecant, one of my classmates asked, "Why should I learn trigonometry when I have a calculator to do that faster and more accurately?"

We've all probably had similar thoughts about moments in life when things just seem meaningless or even absurd and cruel. Some regulations. Selfish thoughtlessness. Microaggressions. A building that collapses and becomes a temporary coffin. People who refuse to vaccinate.

If this post seems grim, it's because on the news the other night we rejoiced with Italy's soccer win just as we feel the pain of Covid-19's newest Delta variant which has now spread to more than two dozen countries.

And yet... we continue to be positive. Not because of wishful thinking, but because of facts and news. Misery might love company but positivity looks for and always finds the good. Always. Maybe that's why "alive and well" appeals to so many people: we persistently invite and challenge our readers to course correct when they feel that life is meaningless, hope is waning or love becomes a struggle.

Lewis Carroll wrote: "If you don't know where you are going, any road will get you there." Translation: when you have a direction and a purpose, it's what keeps you going.

Having a purpose in your life is one of four core dimensions of well-being, along with awareness, connection, and insight... I truly believe it is a crucial key to attaining life satisfaction, which is a more rewarding state than fleeting moments of happiness.

I've mentioned before but it bears repeating that living a meaningful life is linked to better memory, improved cognitive capabilities, a lower risk of heart problems and stroke and so much more.

So, where are you going? Your answer isn't really a place, but rather a <u>space</u>: inner peace, mental freedom, emotional satisfaction, a sense of strong personal moorings. These cannot be given you by a calculator.

Daniel Francis

Correct Me If I'm Wrong

Being Right. I'm not talking about political correctness or all the noise surrounding the so-called "cancel culture." Let's leave out "big lie" concerns or deep fake videos. I want to say that being right as I want to talk about it is not wanting to impress, look smarter or be seen as better informed.

I mean the sincere desire to be correct, accurate and factual. For the sake of truth. For no other reason than to be undergirded by what is authentic and real.

There is no shame in being proven wrong unless the ego feels the pinch.

Who cares where the idea first came from- accept it if it's true. Wouldn't you rather change your mind than hold on to an error, incorrect conclusion or biased opinion based on mere sentiment? Don't suspend good judgment or fail to do appropriate investigation. But do change your opinion if you're wrong.

In some circles, the terms for changing one's mind are "pivot", "evolve" or "upgrade thinking." It doesn't matter what you call it (and some may accuse you of flip-flopping), the important thing is that you are trying to be right, correct your course, steer with a better map. Who doesn't want that?

If truth is more important to me than opining or speaking from the gut, then I will find it easier to listen to and maybe even accept a controversial view.

Let's not care so much about WHO is right; let's prize the truth and make it a value to get things right.

To Give is Amazing

My father's father was born in Italy and baptized Felice Franci. When he came to the USA, like many immigrants he changed his name and was now called Felix Francis.

While I didn't like being teased for having "two first names", I was proud of the statuette of St. Francis that Mom put in the backyard- I found a kinship in him and his love of creation, especially birds.

Years later, I not only have my own backyard statue of the man from Assisi, daily I repeat The Peace Prayer. You know, the one that begins "Lord, make me an instrument of your peace...." Perhaps that prayer inspired this parable:

> Many years ago, a man was sitting in quiet contemplation by a riverbank when he was disturbed by a beggar from the local village.
>
> "Where is the stone?" the beggar demanded. "I must have the precious stone!"
>
> The man smiled up at him. "What stone do you seek?"
>
> "I had a dream," the beggar continued, barely able to slow his words to speak, "and in that dream a voice told me that if I went to the riverbank I would find a man who would give me a precious stone that would end my poverty forever!"
>
> The man looked thoughtful, then reached into his bag and pulled out a large diamond.
>
> "I wonder if this was the stone?" the man said kindly. "I found it on the path. If you'd like it, you may certainly have it."

The beggar couldn't believe his luck, and he snatched the stone from the man's hand and ran back to the village before he could change his mind.

One year later, the beggar, now dressed in the clothes of a wealthy man, came back to the riverbank in search of his anonymous benefactor.

"You have returned, my friend!" said the man, who was again sitting in his favorite spot enjoying the peaceful flow of the water before him. "What has happened?"

The beggar humbled himself before the man.

"Many wonderful things have happened to me because of the diamond you gave me so graciously. I have become wealthy, found a wife and bought a home. I am now able to give employment to others and to do what I want, when I want with whomever I want."

"For what have you returned?" asked the man.

"Please," the rich beggar said. "Teach me whatever it is inside you that allowed you to give me that stone so freely."

(Author Unknown)

Pay Attention

Even if you don't like poetry, you can make your way through these four fabulous lines from Mary Oliver:

Instructions for living a life

Pay attention.

Be astonished.

Tell about it.

See? That wasn't so bad.

What's powerful is that, with an economy of words, Oliver defines the best of social discourse. As humans interact, we can choose to tell so many stories: the regrets of the past, the fears of the future. We can opt to focus on what is going wrong right now with this child or that neighbor, this malady or that politician.

Or, we can tell about what we see and delight in and enjoy... daily, I might add. Who can argue that there is so much about our life on this earth that is nothing short of miraculous?

I'm finishing a book called *Arctic Dreams* by Barry Lopez who spends entire chapters describing the fishing techniques of narwhals or the thundering sound of caribou herds on the move or the dancing lights of the aurora borealis. And this in an area that most of us will never visit.

But I do "astonishment" a disservice if I only speak of wonder and wow as found in nature. Think for a moment about the technology that allows you to read what I've written from my desk to your phone (or laptop) how many thousands of miles away?

Or how about the wonder of the kick of a child in the womb? My two older brothers, strong and macho men, cried at the birth of their firstborns. They cried, too, at the births of the 5th and 6th children, but for different reasons.

Or how about the astonishment so many of us experienced when someone, looking us intimately in the eyes, said "I love you" and sealed those words with a kiss or a ring?

All of this surprise and wonderment is dependent upon one very important capacity: to pay attention. What this requires is to be here now. To be able to take the time to see what it is in front of you, hear who is before you, experience--without judgment or rash opinion--what is happening in your presence.

Finally, tell about it. Share the good news. Fill Facebook and Twitter with the amazement of your life and perhaps you, too, like Mary Oliver, will help people to truly LIVE A LIFE!

Languishing or Adjusting?

The New York Times recently suggested a word for people who are bone-weary of living with the persistent threat of COVID, of avoiding one another, of wearing masks even if you are fully vaccinated out of social solidarity. "It wasn't burnout — we still had energy. It wasn't depression — we didn't feel hopeless. We just felt somewhat joyless and aimless. It turns out there's a name for that: languishing."

The paper goes on to define languishing as a vapid form of stagnation, "as if you're muddling through your days, looking at your life through a foggy windshield."

We know people who are languishing. They understandably miss so much about life

B.C. (Before COVID): they pine for hearty laughs inside restaurants, bear hugs with loved ones, not having glasses fog up due to the requisite mask. They have a boredom that Netflix can't eliminate; they feel an ennui which homemade sourdough bread won't heal; days drag on with a murky longing for a future that seems further away with each new mutation or vaccine side-effect.

While we are aware of the devastatingly negative effects this virus has had on many people since March of 2020, there are some who have discovered their own flexibility-they have been able to make adjustments.

There's the media specialist who has been able to work from home, even preferring being "remote" in sweatpants (during a Zoom call no less) and wondering how she ever dealt with rush hour traffic twice a day or James in accounting.

There's the insurance agent who decides that "enough is

enough" and, taking a good look at his finances, trusts that he can retire and now spend more time with his wife and their garden and Church activities.

Or the young person, introvert by nature and reticent in the classroom, who blossoms online with newly discovered skills in digital technology, writes fearless posts without the worry of blushing or stuttering and enjoys a growing internetwork of friends who don't bully or pressure or compare.

If you are languishing, claim it and name it. It may not change much but at least you'll know that what you are feeling is tied to circumstances mostly outside your control. You are not wrong or weak.

On the other hand, if you are adjusting, know that there are two kinds of adjustments: merely coping or thriving. If you are thriving, please be respectful, patient and sensitive to those who aren't.

But go ahead and relish the way you have used this time to dig (deep) down and make amazing lemonade with what life has given you. And how wonderful if you can wordlessly share that attitude with others.

You are not better or stronger than others. But you are alive and well!

Right Where You Are

I'm haunted by a quote I once read by Robert Pirsig: "The only Zen (peace) you find on tops of mountains is the Zen you bring there."

I'm haunted because it's so tempting to think that going somewhere else (a beautiful mountain lake, a cabin in the woods) can change me on the inside right here. Who doesn't feel more refreshed by beauty, but what happens when you get back home? Why was that change so short-lived?

As David Deida teaches:

> Right now, and in every now-moment, you are either closing or opening. You are either stressfully waiting for something – more money, security, affection – or you are living from your deep heart, opening as the entire moment, and giving what you most deeply desire to give, without waiting.

It's not glamorous, but you can actually do better right where you are. Your situation may lack the grandeur of mountains or the quiet of a cabin, but it could be a very fertile place. How? Watch your behavior today and see how you react to a text, post, phone call, news item, noisy neighbor, careless dog walker, distracted cashier, rude driver....

The truth is, we need people if we are to grow, and all our problems with them, properly seen, are opportunities for growth. Trying to live in harmony with those around you right now will bring out enormous inner toughness.

We are mistaken when we think that peace happens ONLY if something or someone changes (meaning "does

Daniel Francis

what I want"). To summon peace from within when faced
with a stressful experience means that the lake or cabin
become extensions of all that is good in me rather than a
temporary narcotic.

Bring your peace everywhere and you'll be living a
mountaintop experience all the time. Who wouldn't want
that?

Where Are You Going?

I had a routine check-up with my doctor the other day. Despite the fact that the clinic was relatively small, there were a number of doors off the corridors and I was grateful to an attendant for helping to point the way out.

There's a quiet comfort when someone shows you where to go.

The chain of grocery stores where we shop (Publix) is a good example. Often when we ask an employee where a product is, they won't just point to the pasta or paprika section but insist on walking you into that aisle; and many don't leave until you have found the item and might even add, "Is there anything else I can help you with?"

During my college years, I was part of a band for the performance of the musical, *Godspell*. In the musical, a beautiful if haunting song called "By My Side" has the following lyrics:

> Where are you going?
> Where are you going?
> Can you take me with you?
> For my hand is cold
> And needs warmth
> Where are you going?
> Far beyond where the horizon lies
> Where the horizon lies
> And the land sinks into mellow blueness
> Oh please, take me with you.

I think of George Bernard Shaw's quote: "To be in hell is to drift: to be in heaven is to steer."

To any who feel as if you've been adrift for a year, we feel you! It's challenging, if not difficult, to live the way you

Daniel Francis

want when conditions restrict travel, when love means avoiding signs of affection and caution entails avoiding large crowds. We want to steer! Especially as Americans, freedom feels so fake right now. This is my life, right?!

And then I think of the amazing, liberating world of our interior lives. In the deepest, calmest pool of our God-drenched souls there is no struggle, no restriction, nothing conditional.

Perhaps the real issue in life is navigation. As Eknath Easwaran used to teach:

> If your car would only make right-hand turns, would you say that it is free? If it ran around bumping into telephone poles and stop signs, denting fenders and wasting gas, would you ignore it and say, "That's the automotive nature. That's my car's mode of self-expression"? It would take you a long time to get anywhere, and where you arrived would not be up to you.

To get to the clinic for my checkup the other day, I drove two miles and made about 7 turns. If I had a car that did not obey me, I might have ended up in Clearwater Beach-not a bad place to be, but not where I needed to go. It is tragic, but many people's lives are like that.

Just your reading this now tells me something about you-that you want to steer, to be doing and thinking and saying the things that truly represent the best of you.

Isn't that right? If it is, slow down. Begin a practice of starting your day with just 5 minutes of meditation.

To Life!

The Japanese have a word, *ikigai*, which basically means "a life well-lived."

People in parts of that country are well-known (as are other so-called "blue zone" areas) for longevity and a higher degree of happiness.

Walking almost everywhere, rarely retiring from work, enjoying time in their garden, socializing, having small meals with a variety of vegetables and fruits, these are folks who love life and value health and wellness.

Might I suggest that to live life well is also to become a lifelong learner.

School is never out for summer break.

You can never be too old or too good at what you do.

No, school is for life. And life is truly school. Learning is a daily thing, wisdom an endless pursuit.

You never arrive, you never fill up, you never graduate. Because the world is always revealing new lessons...even in the oldest texts.

For example, Seneca wrote many years ago that "there is no one more foolish than one who stops learning."

So be kind to yourself. Take a look at your nutrition, sleep and exercise.

Do a "time audit" every now and then and ask yourself if you are spending your days wisely or wastefully. Do this for you! You have been given the gift of life and the best response is to take care of that gift as well as you can.

Daniel Francis

Keep learning, keep growing, keep stretching, never stop reaching!

Back to those who live in Blue Zone areas, they inspire us to take care of ourselves so that—at the end of our lives— we too may say that we lived an "ikigai" life: well-lived!

What Pandemic?

I find it fascinating that you can jumble the letters in the word *pandemic* to form these words:

encamp   pained   media   dampen   cinema

What's unfortunate is that you can also find the word <u>panic</u> in pandemic.

We saw this early on in our country with blaming and hoarding and fearful overdramatization. People became depressed and were afraid to leave their homes. Focusing on political and racial tensions seemed like a volcanic vent through which to release molten mania.

Thankfully, not everyone has been languishing during this time. Consider this message that came out last year from the senior pastor at North Point Community Church in Alpharetta, Georgia:

> Sometimes I just want it to stop. Talk of COVID, looting, brutality. I lose my way. I become convinced that this 'new normal' is real life.

> Then I meet an 87-year-old who talks of living through polio, diphtheria, Vietnam protests and yet is still enchanted with life. He seemed surprised when I said 2020 must be especially challenging for him.

>> 'No,' he said slowly, looking me straight in the eyes. 'I learned a long time ago to not see the world through the printed headlines, I see the world through the people that surround me.

>> I see the world with the realization that

Daniel Francis

we love big. Therefore, I just choose to
write my own headlines: 'Husband loves
wife today.' 'Family drops everything to
come to Grandma's bedside.'

He patted my hand. 'Old man makes new
friend.'

His words collide with my worries, freeing them
from the tether I had been holding tight. They
float away. I am left with a renewed spirit and a
new way to write my own headlines.

- Andy Stanley

Yes, I shout (can you hear me?)! This kind of new
narrative is what Alive 'n Well is all about! To unburden
ourselves (sometimes peel off band aids that haven't been
necessary for a while) and live into a new, more healthy
present and future!

Not to dismiss reality nor ignore societal sins or national
issues... but to hear this positivity from a man who has
lived through so much negativity is inspiring!!! Okay, I'm
running out of exclamation points, but you get the idea.

Finally, "there are two ways of spreading light: to be the
candle or the mirror that reflects it" (Edith Wharton).

Which one do I want to be? Which one am I? If I need to
change, what's stopping me?

Seeing I to Eye

A dear friend recently gave us a beautiful drawing which includes part of a quote from Rumi:

Out beyond ideas of wrongdoing and rightdoing, there is a
field.
I'll meet you there.

The origin of the word *reconciliation* comes from the concept of seeing eyelash to eyelash (cilia). To be con-cilia means to literally get eyelash to eyelash with someone; when you reconcile you are returning to seeing "eye to eye."

Did you catch the Oscars earlier this year? One of the finest moments was when Tyler Perry accepted the Jean Hersholt Humanitarian Award with these words:

> My mother taught me to refuse hate. She taught me to refuse blanket judgment... I refuse to hate someone because they're Mexican or because they are black or white, or LGBTQ. I refuse to hate someone because they're a police officer. I refuse to hate someone because they are Asian. I would hope that we would refuse hate.

Perry's speech reminded me of a story:

> A long, long ago, there lived two brothers who loved each other very much. They were poor wheat farmers, and they shared but one field, which yielded very little harvest during the year. The younger brother lived on one side of the field in a two-room house with his wife and children, and the older brother lived alone in a one-room house on the opposite side of the field.

One night during harvest-time, the older brother awoke suddenly. He sat up in his bed, thinking, It's not fair that I should receive an equal share of the wheat with my brother. He should have a greater share because he has a wife and children to feed besides himself. It must be very difficult for him, yet he never complains.

So the older brother got up from his bed, dressed, and went out to where he kept his wheat. It took him several trips across the dark field to carry a goodly portion of his wheat to his brother's wheat pile. When he returned home, he slept peacefully the rest of the night.

Later that same night the younger brother awoke suddenly. He sat up in his bed, thinking, It's not fair that I should receive an equal share of the wheat with my brother. I have a wife and children. When I grow old, I will have someone to care for me, to provide food for me. My brother has no children. When he grows old, he will be alone. He should have the greater share of the wheat so that he can sell some of it to provide for his old age.

So the younger brother got up from his bed, dressed, and went out to where he kept his wheat. It took him several trips across the dark field to carry a goodly portion of his wheat to his brother's wheat pile. When he returned home, he slept peacefully the rest of the night. The next day each brother looked in amazement at his own pile of wheat, only to discover that it had not diminished!

The brothers again worked in the field, divided the wheat, and added wheat to each other's pile during the night. And so it continued for many nights during the harvest.

One night as the older brother was carrying his wheat across the field, he saw his younger brother carrying his wheat across the field.

They stopped and looked at each other and at what the other one was carrying. Then they understood why the wheat piles never grew smaller.

They both realized how much they loved and cared for each other.

The brothers dropped their bundles of wheat to the ground, ran to each other, and embraced.

God saw the love that these brothers had for each other. He blessed their field, and the field became more and more fertile.

The brothers grew much wheat together, enough for both to live on when they grew older.

The remainder of the quote from Rumi goes:

When the soul lies down in that grass, the world is too full to talk about.

Whether on the street, at the grocers, online, in Facebook or Twitter, may you meet others--even if you strongly disagree with them--in the open field.

I promise you that you will see eye to eye when the ego leaves and acceptance fills your countenance.

Daniel Francis

Dormant

A few weeks ago, my reflection referenced a word for people who are not doing well during this time, *languishing*. Not too long afterward, another word has surfaced as a sort of rebuttal to the idea that people are aimless and joyless: dormant.

The author, Austin Kleon, writes:

> I disliked the term "languishing" the minute I heard it.
> I'm not languishing, I'm dormant.
> Like a plant.
> Or a volcano.
> I am waiting to be activated.

Kleon writes about how being married to a gardener gives him rich metaphors for understanding time which goes by another clock- Mother Nature. As he says,

> Gardeners not only develop a different sense of time, they develop the ancient wisdom of knowing when to do things: To every thing there is a season, and a time to every purpose under the heaven: A time to be born, and a time to die; a time to plant, and a time to pluck up that which is planted; A time to kill, and a time to heal; a time to break down, and a time to build up... ...if you try to wake a plant out of dormancy too soon, it will wither, and maybe die.
> - Like the butterfly whose final stage can't be rushed before it takes wing.
> - Like a broken bone that needs time to heal.
> - Like the dormant bear whose den is not merely for waiting but for nurturing her cubs.

Corita Kent described her own dormant stretches saying that "new things are happening very quietly inside of me."

As my bride and I continue to tend our garden this Spring, already jasmine and gardenia have scented the air, Easter Lilies trumpeted their flowers, orchids are boasting their buds and lilies of the Nile are popping up like papyrus.

Nature continues to bust open (spring forth!) and all in Her own time.

Daniel Francis

What, A Pain?

It was the summer after I graduated from 6th grade. Going to "middle school" felt so mature. I remember having a conversation with a cute girl down the street who was in my class. She was taller than I and more adult sounding, so I looked up to her in both ways. I can't remember what we spoke about but it had tones of "Now that we're grown up..." or "Since we won't have recess anymore"... you know, that kind of pre-teen sophistication.

As an introvert, going to a new school and befriending new classmates was scary. It's just one of the many rites of passage that all of us had to go through, probably with various levels of eagerness, enjoyment, enthusiasm or--like me--trepidation!

But oh! to be able to exchange the growing pains of our childhood and teen years for the burdens of adulthood with bills, insurance, doctors, divorce, death of friends... the list goes on.

And then there are wisdom figures, spiritual leaders, even accidental conversations that give us a change of heart, a mind modification.

For example, the singer, Jewel, writes in *Never Broken*:

> You can't outrun your pain. You are strong enough to face whatever is in front of you. Medicating your pain will only bring more pain. The only genuine shortcut life offers is facing your feelings. They won't kill you. Feelings are your soul's way of communicating. Pain is trying to teach you something, and if you don't listen now, it will speak louder and louder until it is heard.

Create Connections

I saw a Ted talk the other day that made me marvel at how two people can go through similar experiences and come out with different interpretations.

The video was of a Mr. Eddie Jaku who describes himself as the "happiest man on earth" (he's now 101).

Quite a boast considering he was sent to Auschwitz, lost most of his family and saw death too often throughout World War II. But, because he managed to survive, he made a vow to smile every day.

I don't believe in luck, but what I know for sure (as I've experienced countless times in my own life) is that when you look for what you need, you begin to see possibilities, probabilities, solutions and successes.

If it's not the exact thing you need, it will eventually help you get to what you need. Connections happen; people appear; assistance is provided.

If you want more to go on, read this quote from David Hoffman, longtime film director:

> It seems to me that when I have a positive view towards anything, a positive result will more likely occur. Now being 79 years old and living a life that 99% of the time was spectacular, I've proven my theory over and over again.

I want to be clear. I don't believe in the Power of Attraction so much as the power of positivity. If you want to be mad and mean, angry and agitated, you'll find lots of ways and reasons to remain that way. Remember that if you are a hammer, you're often looking for a nail to hit.

Daniel Francis

But when your lens changes, what seems magical happens
and life just aligns to give you what you need... and
sometimes you are given exactly what you want, too!

Use Those Muscles

Have you ever wondered why many people smile when they are taking someone else's picture? Due mainly to the zygomaticus major which gets pulled at an angle superolaterally, we use between 17 and 43 muscles to smile.

That said, do you remember the last time you laughed so hard your face hurt? What a joy that pain is!

I remember a colleague telling me about an international conference he went to which was held in Italy. It was in the early 90s, not too long after the end of the Cold War and the Berlin Wall had been brought down.

Some participants were from East Berlin. The morning after the opening gala, one of the Germans said he could barely sleep because he heard the others laughing into the wee hours. They apologized but he quickly stopped them. "No," he said. "It was wonderful. I hadn't heard such laughter in years!"

The home office where Alice and I work is happily near a window overlooking our front yard. For some years, we would see a woman passing our house along the sidewalk; we named her "The Smiler" as there was truly no other way to describe the happy grin on her face.

When we were out walking one afternoon she neared us and I blurted out, "We call you the smiling woman." Her smile only increased. Unfortunately for us, she moved two years ago. I can only hope that wherever she now calls home there are others who benefit and appreciate her persistent smile.

One final quote: "Empathy is about finding echoes of another person in yourself" (Mohsin Hamid).

Daniel Francis

Hey, if they say yawning is contagious, perhaps when we smile we might make someone reach inside and do the same.

I think the world would be better off, don't you!?

Flight Risk

Before you read the following quote, I have a confession
to make. Seeing some of the "flight fights" that have been
occurring with angry passengers assaulting flight attendants
or other seatmates had me recall my time in the air.

When I was giving talks across the country and flew 2 to 3
times a month, I am ashamed to admit that I would
sometimes let people in terminals and in the air unnerve
me, take my peace away, hijack my stillness.

For example, I vividly recall with not a little
embarrassment wrangling for the armrest shared by the
woman seated next to me. Once I established my part of
that tiny elbow real estate, I got back to what I was
reading: *Peace Is Every Step* by Thich Nhat Hanh. Oops!

Ryan Holiday captures this well:

> The people on your flight tomorrow will be slow
> and rude. They will recline their seats into you.
> They will clog the aisles. They will watch videos
> on their phone without earbuds in. They will fight
> you for the armrests, even though they obviously
> belong to the person in the middle seat.
>
> They will take too long in the bathroom. And
> they will do ungodly things in there while they're
> at it. They will take forever to deplane; they will
> not care that half the plane have connections to
> make.
> They will do all these things, without fail, and no
> amount of frustrated muttering, anxiety,
> impatience, and dirty looks will fix it.
> Do you understand that? This is just how it is.
>
> The real question is why? They are like this

because they are flawed people. Because they don't fly as much as you. Because they are dealing with their own anxiety and worries, because maybe they have had a nightmare of a trip so far, because they have their own connection to make.

Being trapped in a thin metal tube, 35,000 feet above the earth with a diverse collection of humanity and no escape is not always fun. And sometimes it does not bring out the best in people.

It goes without saying that you don't have to fly the blue skies to encounter a black cloud created by an angry person online or in line. You can't control what they do or say.

You can, however, control how you deal with it- it's totally up to you to let what is occurring outside of you to pass through you. You do not have to let it "stick".

Let your craw be for nutritional food and not the junk or funk of someone else's drama.

Subtract to Add

A number of years ago, I was having dinner in a restaurant with a colleague of mine. Bill was 30 years my senior and he had just found out that a good friend of his died.

At one point during the meal, he began to weep quietly... and then he looked at me and sighed, "I truly believe that I know more people in heaven than on earth."

When my parents moved to Florida in 1991, my mom used to say she was going to God's green room (in talk show verbiage, that's the name of the place guests wait before they go on stage)... a humorous way of describing her post-retirement life before God would call her.

I'm grateful that she had 10 years to enjoy the garden, warmth and new friends she made in the sunshine state.

And now here I am closer to 60 than 50 and AARP has been sending me lots of stuff! The older I get the more I realize that one aspect of life is about letting go.

- Letting go of junk you'll never use
- Letting go of friends who don't call back
- Letting go of old ideas that maybe were never, ever any good (!)
- Letting go of old grievances and stale regrets
- Letting go of judgment and opinions that only feed the ego

Did you ever hear that sad and empty saying used among consumeristic competitive people: "The one who dies with the most toys wins!"

Perhaps we can learn from the dilemma babies have when they have learned to hold but not release: in one hand they grip a rattle and then you offer them a cheerio. For a while they look back and forth at the rattle and then at the cereal. You can visualize their mind processing wanting the food but not being able to with their hand full.

I've heard of a certain type of monkey that is easy to catch. You only have to put peanuts into a hole smaller than the size of its closed fist. Once the monkey smells the delight, it sticks a hand in, grabs ahold of the peanuts but can't pull its arm out for the size of the hole; the trapper can then transfer it to another area of the park.

Author Neale Donald Walsh once wrote, "You cannot let go of anything if you cannot notice that you are holding it."

St. Francis says that unless we do our first death now (grieving our losses and failures and imperfections), the second death (our bodily one) will be very difficult.

Here's to practicing letting go now so that we can honor and love those we've lost while also living as fully as we can now.

Accepting What Is... Mostly

There was a tradition in my family on Sundays.

After going to Church, we'd come home and my father would cook us delicious breakfast for lunch: either pancakes or French toast. And always accompanying his cooking would be music at high volume coming from the Grundig stereo.

Gifted with a good voice, Dad would be crooning to "Born Too Late" by the Pony-Tails or "How Much is That Doggie in the Window" by Patti Page or "Zing! Went the Strings of My Heart" by the Coasters. You remember those songs, right?

One of the tunes which would get us all swinging and swaying was Doris Day's "Que Sera Sera", with the words:

> Que sera, sera
> Whatever will be, will be
> The future's not ours to see
> Que sera, sera
> What will be, will be

Now, as a life coach I'm constantly reminding people not to fight with reality... because reality always wins! You can name what's in front of you as a problem, an obstacle or an enemy, but it is real.

And yet... To accept what is does not mean that you don't participate in life, that you don't take action as needed. True acceptance does not equal resignation or putting up with things that are not okay. Why?

We are agents of change. If something is not working for you, if the way you are living is not aligning with your values and priorities, what are you waiting for? Yes, the future might not be "ours to see", but we can change what happens in the future by making significant corrections in our present.

I don't know what that means for you. I just know that reality is not a threat; on the contrary, it can be a messenger that reminds you to write YOUR story going forward.

"... As To Understand..."

I came upon a quote from artist, author and photographer, Doe Zantamata, which truly made me pause and think:

> It's easy to judge. It's more difficult to understand. Understanding requires compassion, patience, and a willingness to believe that good hearts sometimes choose poor methods. Through judging, we separate. Through understanding, we grow.

I'm not sure I've seen it clearer than this: judging separates; understanding helps us grow. I hope you notice that nothing in this tells us to agree blindly with someone or adopt their opinion or accept their point of view.

What it does is challenge us to honor where they stand and recognize how they feel. And if it makes you feel better, perhaps you, too, quickly think of the quote by Daniel Patrick Moynihan, "Everyone is entitled to their own opinion but not their own facts."

Richard Rohr continually writes about the sad need for the small mind to lump people into categories, separating those who think one way away from "my" group. What this does is encamp ideologies of right and wrong so that "those-over-there" will only be acceptable once they agree with my position and take my side. This is the small mind.

The broad mind, however, allows space to listen and learn, disagree when that's appropriate, but never demean, dismiss or disassociate.

I've got a long way to go, but I find teachers (and classrooms) everywhere.

Anyone else feel this way?

Daniel Francis

More wisdom from Doe Zantamata:

- You cannot convince someone to see something that they do not want to see, no matter how much you know it would improve their lives.
- You have to love and accept them exactly as they are today. If you cannot do that, you have to let them go and find their own way, in their own time, if they ever choose to do so. Otherwise, you'll be giving them the power over your happiness, too.
- Your intuition is the most honest friend that you will ever have.
- Your inner spark never dies.
- Quiet your mind enough to feel it again.
- Once you do, it will begin to ignite.
- Sometimes people confuse self-love with big ego. The two are totally different. A person with a big ego thinks they are better than others. A person who loves him or herself doesn't think they are better or worse than others.
- Comparing is useless, as we all have strengths and weaknesses. Focusing on one or the other is not the whole picture.
- If you love yourself, you know you are worthy of love, of good things in life, and that you are capable of unlimited great things.
- You will inspire others to realize the same about themselves as well.

Are You In Or Out?

When I was 19, I went to a college graduation of friends of mine. In a crowd of perhaps 600, I knew barely 20 people and at the luncheon afterward I needed to "escape." It was the first time in my life that I realized I was an introvert.

That might sound funny and unlikely for someone who is comfortable with public speaking (I've given conferences and talks on four continents) and zoominars; but the truth is that to "recharge my batteries", I need to step AWAY from the crowd.

For extroverts, typically it's the opposite- they go TO parties and bars in order to get energized.

With our country almost fully "opened up" in most places, it must be quite a breath of fresh air to many, especially extroverts.

There is another category on the personality spectrum and it's called ambiversion- someone who is between introversion and extroversion. Where are you?

No matter what "vert" you are, just like belly buttons-- outies and innies--there is no better one.

However you orient yourself, the important thing is to know what zaps or renews your strength.

Daniel Francis

A Memorable Day

The tears fell.

It always happens.

Every year, we watch the *National Memorial Day Concert* on PBS.

What moves us is when actors tell the stories of the heroes through the memories and messages of their loved ones. The accounts of bravery, courage, indefatigable love of country, protecting our freedom and all that the United States of America stands for... just opens a floodgate of appreciation and pride.

That's it from me. Now read on for profound quotes from great minds:

> "This nation will remain the land of the free only so long as it is the home of the brave."
> – Elmer Davis

> "No man is entitled to the blessings of freedom unless he be vigilant in its preservation."
> – General Douglas MacArthur

> "Heroism doesn't always happen in a burst of glory. Sometimes small triumphs and large hearts change the course of history."
> – Mary Roach

> "It doesn't take a hero to order men into battle. It takes a hero to be one of those men who goes into battle."
> – Norman Schwarzkopf

> "Patriotism is not short, frenzied outbursts of

emotion, but the tranquil and steady dedication of a lifetime."
— Adlai Stevenson

"America without her soldiers would be like God without His angels."
— Claudia Pemberton

"I believe our flag is more than just cloth and ink. It is a universally recognized symbol that stands for liberty, and freedom. It is the history of our nation, and it's marked by the blood of those who died defending it."
— John Thune

"The willingness of America's veterans to sacrifice for our country has earned them our lasting gratitude."
— Jeff Miller

"I have long believed that sacrifice is the pinnacle of patriotism."
— Bob Riley

"There is nothing nobler than risking your life for your country."
— Nick Lampson

"Over all our happy country over all our Nation spread, is a band of noble heroes—is our Army of the Dead."
— Will Carleton

"What I can do for my country, I am willing to do."
— Christopher Gadsden

Daniel Francis

"A hero is someone who has given his or her life to something bigger than oneself."
– Joseph Campbell

"It is foolish and wrong to mourn the men who died. Rather we should thank God such men lived."
– George S. Patton

"In the End, we will remember not the words of our enemies, but the silence of our friends."
– Martin Luther King, Jr.

"I only regret that I have but one life to lose for my country."
– Nathan Hale

"I love America more than any other country in the world, and exactly for this reason, I insist on the right to criticize her perpetually."
– James A. Baldwin

"Patriotism is supporting your country all the time, and your government when it deserves it."
– Mark Twain

"My fellow Americans, ask not what your country can do for you, ask what you can do for your country."
– John F. Kennedy

"You will never do anything in this world without courage."
– Aristotle

"Never was so much owed by so many few."
– Winston Churchill

"A hero is someone who understands the
responsibility that comes with his freedom."
– Bob Dylan

"Freedom makes a huge requirement of every
human being. With freedom comes
responsibility."
– Eleanor Roosevelt

"Those who have long enjoyed such privileges as
we enjoy forget in time that men have died to win
them."
– Franklin D. Roosevelt

"Never throughout history has a man who lived a
life of ease left a name worth remembering."
– Theodore Roosevelt

"Without memory, there is no culture. Without
memory there would be no civilization, no
future."
– Elie Wiesel

Daniel Francis

No Regrets

There's a scene in the Academy Award-winning movie,
Nomadland, when a woman explains her decision to live life
by being nomadic- taking her motor home and moving
around to see the country as she pleases, where she desires:

> I worked for corporate America, you know, for
> twenty years. And my friend, Bill, worked for the
> same company, and he had liver failure.

> A week before he was due to retire, HR called him
> in hospice, and said, "Now, let's talk about your
> retirement." And he died ten days later, having
> never been able to take that sailboat that he
> bought out of his driveway.

> And he missed out on everything. And he told
> me before he died, "Just don't waste any time,
> Merle. Don't waste any time."

> So I retired as soon as I could. I didn't want my
> sailboat to be in the driveway when I died. So,
> yeah. And it's not. My sailboat's out here in the
> desert.

I do not condone living hedonistically nor thoughtlessly.
But I heartfully applaud anyone who lives life fully,
intentionally and lovingly... especially with abandon. And
when doing so benefits others, all the better!

Lucille Ball once said, "I'd rather regret the things I've
done than regret the things I hadn't done." Studies indicate
that fear of failing outranks regret, but that's not true when
you talk to someone facing death.

As Brian Clark writes in *Further*, the wise elderly and
terminally ill confess that they wish they had taken more

chances.

After all, when you're facing death, you're acutely aware that this life is not a dress rehearsal. And yet, we are often the biggest impediment to our own happiness by clinging to self-limiting beliefs.

At the end of this first week of the sixth month of 2021, there's no room for past regrets or guilt. My hope is that we have acknowledged mistakes we've made in the past and that we can use them as lessons to become kinder, gentler, more mature people.

Intelligence vs. Wisdom

We've all seen examples of so-called "nutty professors." People who have an amazing amount of book knowledge but can't remember where the car keys are; they can explain non-fungible tokens and nanotechnology yet forget their spouse's birthday.

I once wanted to know the contents of all the books in our college library (I was a budding philosopher after all) and one of my professors said that it would be a waste of space in my head.

"Ask yourself," he continued, "why they wrote the books and those answers will make you wise."

So here goes. I don't know the source of this list but it's chock-full of... wait for it... wisdom!

1. Intelligence leads to arguments. Wisdom leads to settlements.

2. Intelligence is power of will. Wisdom is power OVER will.

3. Intelligence is heat, it burns. Wisdom is warmth, it comforts.

4. Intelligence is pursuit of knowledge, it tires the seeker. Wisdom is pursuit of truth, it inspires the seeker.

5. Intelligence is holding on. Wisdom is letting go.

6. Intelligence leads you. Wisdom guides you.

7. An intelligent woman thinks she knows everything. A wise woman knows that there is still something to learn.

8. An intelligent man always tries to prove his point. A wise man knows there really is no point.

9. An intelligent person freely gives unsolicited advice. A wise person keeps her counsel until all options are considered.

10. An intelligent person understands what is being said. A wise person understands what is left unsaid.

11. An intelligent woman speaks when she has to say something. A wise woman speaks when she has something to say.

12. An intelligent man sees everything as relative. A wise man sees everything as related.

13. An intelligent person tries to control the mass flow. A wise person navigates the mass flow.

14. An intelligent man preaches. A wise woman reaches.

Bottom Line: Intelligence is good but wisdom achieves better results.

Daniel Francis

Father's Day Weekend- Memories

"It's called a lug nut," my dad said to me.

As a Navy Chief, his dress whites were immaculate. This day, though, his hands were darkened from the oil and grease that caked the wheel and wrench and the big, heavy metallic objects he asked me to put down one at a time as he changed the flat tire. "You have to put them back on evenly."

One of seven children and the last of four boys, dad was both teaching me and saving money. He knew the gas station charged "an arm and a leg" to tow the car and do the job. He would do it himself, thank you very much. I had seen him a few times showing my older brothers about how to make sure the parking brake was engaged, that you jacked up the car after you loosened the nuts.

This day, however, they and my sisters were not around, and I was happy that he (pretended to) need my assistance for this job. I cherished these rare learning moments.

Twenty-plus years later as I was finishing a business trip in Florida, I made plans to visit my parents who had just moved there a few years before. It was Sunday and I was in the middle of the state among orange groves and strawberry farms that sprawled forever. The beauty was calming. But as I was about an hour from their house, the back left tire flattened. This was before good cell phones and reliable reception. A.A.A. was out of the question and no cars were headed in either direction.

So yes, in my early 30s, for the first time in my life I had to do some auto mechanistry. Remembering as much of the DIY my dad had taught me (admittedly, I also used the guide in the rental car's manual), I did it- I changed a flat tire! Some say you're not a man until you have a child, publish a book or plant a tree. I say it happened on Florida State Road 555 to a smiling fool holding a tire iron... proud of stained hands and a sweaty shirt.

When I pulled in to my parents' home and regaled the story, dad was proud; mom rolled her eyes in mock teasing. We laughed and enjoyed a wonderful meal.

After mom died, dad's mind began to falter. We knew he missed her, but he was also missing other things- appointments, keys and then inhibition, names and words. The diagnosis was almost certainly Alzheimer's, we were told.

One day, while taking him to the bathroom after I fed him, it occurred to me that there was no manual to fix my dad's flattened mind. I was now like a father to him and, perhaps for the second time in my life, became a man.

Daddy, you're gone now 8 years, but your patience and love, together with mom's wisdom and strength, are the wheels in my life that keep me going.

[This story first appeared at www.insidewink.com.]

Daniel Francis

Choosing Not To Opine

As a wedding officiant, I invite the couple to choose a reading or two for their ceremony. A favorite is the beautiful passage from 1st Corinthians with the message that "love is patient; love is kind...."

What I've noticed throughout this past year is that another common wedding selection from Ecclesiastes is particularly appropriate for all of us: "there is a time to speak and a time to keep silent."

Years ago the Roman Emperor Marcus Aurelius wrote: "We have the power to hold no opinion about a thing and to not let it upset our state of mind—for things have no natural power to shape our judgments."

Imagine. We have the power not to have an opinion. That doesn't mean that we agree with everything or ignore what we believe to be wrong or even evil.

But why get so upset? Why stress out over things or people that you cannot control. Since our energy is finite, the question is "How are we going to spend it?" Are we looking online for ego-stroking affirmation by convincing people that our "side" is the correct one? Do we relish arguments for the sake of winning over someone? Can we be okay keeping quiet and not needing to express ourselves always?

Please believe that I know how hypocritical this sounds coming from someone who writes two reflections a week!

But think about it: to choose not to share an opinion is absolutely freeing and humbling. It's freeing because I don't have to CLING to my thinking and fortify my castle and prepare my defenses; it's humbling in that most people probably don't care what I think anyway. That's not something to take personally- it's just the truth. Folks just have more important things to do than being cajoled or persuaded by ideology or philosophy or opinions.

Back to the opening image... perhaps more couples might benefit from knowing when to speak and when to stay quiet.

Daniel Francis

eMotion Sickness

On this final Friday of July, I want to share something that caught my coach's heart a few weeks ago.

As I was reading through material I get for assisting clients on their journey, I came upon a phrase that was both clever and true: "emotional sickness".

We all know what happens to some people who literally get sick to their stomach in a car or carnival ride and we call this motion sickness, "caused by a mismatch in the cues coming from your eyes, your vestibular (balance) system and the movement sensors in your brain."

But what is emotional sickness (a word coined by singer Phoebe Bridgers)?

Well, let's go back to the carnival example. When you are on a roller coaster ride of ups and downs that make you angry one day and awestruck another; elated then worried; fascinated then bored out of your mind; apoplectic one minute and grateful the next... you'll soon suffer from emotional sickness. And, similar to car sickness, you can get sick to the stomach.

So what to do when joy and jitters get to you in the same day, sometimes within the same hour? "Relax and release" as Michael Singer is fond of saying.

- Relax. Watching your emotions can immediately help to distance them. You can even say to yourself, "I feel anger but I am NOT my anger." See yourself as if from across the room and say, "This will not last." You know this is true because you have a lifetime of experiences which back this up. What you are feeling will pass.

- Release. Not to cling to your emotions--whether positive or negatives--keeps that space open for this moment now. Releasing allows you to unburden yourself from what never belonged to you in the first place: fleeting feelings which only drag you into regret or nostalgia... and keep you from living in the present.

Might I be so bold as to ask: what is your dominant emotional state? How (who) are you when you are not experiencing ups and downs? Where does your balance come from? When you can answer this question, you have your own Dramamine for stabilizing your mind and enjoying the ride!

Daniel Francis

Don't Let Fear Be A Factor

Last month I wrote about planning for enjoyable moments
in the future:

Think about it: When you have tickets in your hand for a
concert or sports event, they're merely pieces of cellulose
wood pulp we call paper, but they give us access to
tremendous joy. A small metallic key is not the car but it
literally opens the door to our "wheels." A ring in a felt
box means nothing without the love and commitment
signified by the giver's smile and bended knee. You get
the idea.

On the opposite end of the mood spectrum is feeling
anxiety or fear now. Think of stage fright which typically
occurs BEFORE the curtains open or the spotlight is on
you. People who have a fear of heights know they're
probably not going to fall off the cliff...but the
POSSIBILITY of it happening makes their palms moist
and legs limp.

We allow negative, future possibilities to hijack our present
peace.

As Ryan Holiday asks, "Why are you borrowing
unhappiness? Why would you be miserable now just
because you might be in the future?"

This doesn't mean not to prepare or plan. However, if you
look for negative things to happen, many times you'll find
them. But when you anticipate finding something
amazing, you'll be astonished at how right you are more
times than not!

Beginner's Heart

When I was working in East Harlem in the early 90s, I attended a conference on community building and grass-roots movements. Inspired to act for change, I blurted out to a staff member, "I think I now understand this stuff."

Sister Regina, 30 years my senior, gently reprimanded me: "Be careful, because there is always more to learn."

This is similar to a Zen phrase known as "beginner's mind." I'm not a Buddhist, but I find it encouraging that in every moment we can begin again.

I heard an interview with an actor who described growing up as an Army brat: "Every year or two, we were in a different zip code. But the disadvantages weighed less than the positives. For instance, I made new friends often and no one knew my past. I could begin over and over again with each new kid and every new school."

If you deal with new situations by listening to old tapes, you might be missing out on a lot!

Kids call them "do overs" or they simply press the reset button on a video game. Know this: you can always begin again.

And what's better than a beginner's mind? A beginner's heart.

A beginner's heart is the fresh feeling that no matter what has happened in my past "I got this", "I'm on course", "I'm made for this."

While a beginner's mind is helpful for removing judgment and the poison of the past, a beginner's heart helps you feel the rightness, the goodness and the notion that "All is well" (Julian of Norwich)."

Daniel Francis

Peace

Outside our guestroom window is a reminder. We made a Peace Pole. It has four sides which Alice painted to reflect our mutual ancestry: part Spanish (her), part Italian and Slovak (me) and American.

The Peace Pole Project was started in Japan by Masahisa Goi (1916 – 1980), who dedicated his life to spreading the message, "May Peace Prevail on Earth".

Mr. Goi was greatly affected by the destruction caused by World War II and the atomic bombs which fell on the cities of Hiroshima and Nagasaki.

For us, the pole is a reminder of what has been planted in us by our parents, from our spirituality as well as our combined learning and growing through the years.

The following is a story which illustrates peace in a stirring way:

> There was once a queen who offered a prize to the artist who could paint the best picture of peace. Many artists tried. The queen looked at all the pictures. After much deliberation, she was down to the last two. She had to choose between them.

> One picture was of a calm lake. The lake was a perfect mirror for the peaceful mountains that towered around it. Fluffy white clouds floated overhead in a blue sky. Everyone who saw this picture remarked at the tranquility of the scenery.

> The second picture had beautifully drawn mountains, too. But these mountains were rugged and bare. Above was an angry sky from which

rain fell and lightning flashed. Down the side of
the mountain tumbled a foaming waterfall. This
did not appear to be a peaceful place at all.

But, when the queen looked closer, she saw that
behind the waterfall was a tiny bush growing in
the rock. Within the branches, a bird had built a
nest. There in the midst of the rush of angry
water, sat the mother bird on her nest.

The queen chose this picture as the perfect picture
of peace. "Peace", she explained, "is not only in a
place where there is no noise, trouble or hard
work. Peace is in the midst of things as they are,
when there is calm in your heart."

Who or what do you allow to diminish or kidnap your
peace? What if your peace was generated from within and
not something that relied on outside experiences?

Imagine how free you would feel about things that
normally bother you! It IS possible to attain this peace-
for you have it inside, just buried perhaps by too many
years of disappointment and anger.

Daniel Francis

Remember or Imagine

When I volunteered at an assisted living home during my college years, I noticed that the senior citizens I visited with could be classified more or less into two groups: those who were nostalgic and spoke almost exclusively of the past and those who were looking ahead.

The first group seemed sadder as they remembered people who were long gone, places they wished they had visited or things they could no longer do.

The second group by and large were friendlier and happier, expressing enthusiasm about the world, the next meal, a relative coming to visit or even the weather.

In 1971, Carly Simon sang "We can never know about the days to come/But we think about them anyway"(from the song *Anticipation*).

To be sure, no one can predict the future (even meteorologists have a tough time). But tomorrow can be crafted by what you plan to do with it.

Sounds too simple and basic? And yet the truth is that many people let things happen to them. Why?

As Brian Clark explains, when we think about who we are in the present, we're really thinking about the past: Our memories of the past, whether good or bad, dominate our brains.

Of course, we know the past is gone and so is the person who experienced that past. The reason why true change is so hard is because even though we logically know the past doesn't control our future, we stay mired in it anyway.

Don't beat yourself up about it, because that's how our brains are wired.

When you force yourself to imagine instead of defaulting to remembering you shift your identity to the type of person you want to be.

Here are the steps:

- Accept the good, important work of creating your future self now; be proactive
- Imagine the specifics: see yourself doing what you want to be doing
- Map out the steps that will allow you to get to where you want to be
- Change is going to happen. Do you want to be acted upon by default or help to architect the future?

Ah yes, these are truly the good old days.

And knowing that can change how you view your life now.

Daniel Francis

Risky Business

First story:

> A mother switched off the light and said
> goodnight, but her daughter broke into tears,
> sobbing "Don't leave me, Mommy!" The mother
> tried to reassure her daughter: "There's nothing to
> be afraid of in the darkness, for God is with you!"
> The girl paused for a moment and replied, "Yes,
> but I need someone with skin on!"

In our neighborhood, there are quite a number of young
families and children. And when a car goes racing down
the street I often say to my wife, "They must have to go to
the bathroom."

I try and give the driver the benefit of the doubt as I can't
imagine anyone risking harm to a pedestrian or other
driver just for a need for speed or sheer impatience.

All of which brings me to the whole vaccination and mask-
wearing issue.

Why is it an issue? If we love our neighbor (didn't
someone once command us to do that), how could we
knowingly jeopardize them when a jab or a piece of cloth
could mean the difference between life and sickness or
even death?

How did the health of our nation and world become
muddied in a false debate about freedom vs. bodily
autonomy, government vs. overreach, safety vs. the
economy?

It pains me to wonder why there is so much mistrust of
one another in the name of politics or party loyalty?

I don't think there's a more persuasive argument than the

one I heard recently from a doctor who compares anti-vaxxers to individuals who are allowed to drink as much alcohol as they want at home and not risk arrest; however, the moment they get behind the wheel of a car they are committing a crime (and a sin in Catholic moral theology) by willfully endangering themselves and others through the possibility of vehicular manslaughter.

Second story:

> An upset man approached the holy Rabbi Ba'al Shem Tov pleading, "My son is estranged from God; what shall I do?" The rabbi replied simply, "Love him more."

Back to me... Okay. I'll try. As I've said in these reflections before: the way forward is usually very simple but rarely easy.

In the meantime, folks: get a vaccine if you haven't already; mask up if you care about those who are vulnerable; and join me in trying to have the skin of God and the wisdom of an old rabbi.

Daniel Francis

Honey As Vinegar

A while ago, we bought some honey for tea. I noticed that the label proclaims: "Raw and Unfiltered." A google search reports that these two qualities of honey make it:

- a good source of antioxidants
- full of antibacterial and antifungal properties
- a phytonutrient powerhouse
- an aid for digestive issues

However, in conversations online, on the phone or at the checkout line, "raw and unfiltered" may lead to "foot-in-mouth" disease. Quick comebacks might score verbal points for speedy wit, but rarely do they reflect the peace that is our natural state. How do I know peace is our natural state?

Think about the last time you had a moment of inspiration, joy, beauty or bliss: a serene lake, the colors of a twilight sky, a baby's smile, the quiet on a trail. These encounters touch us deeply precisely because what we are taking in from outside is mirroring what we feel and know deep within. It's our native disposition.

T.S. Eliot writes in Little Gidding:

> We shall not cease from exploration
> And the end of all our exploring
> Will be to arrive where we started
> And know the place for the first time.

There are "aha" moments with my coaching clients when they realize that most of the questions they were asking had been answered throughout their lives in varying circumstances. Their native instinct lets them "arrive" home to their inner wisdom.

At first, to filter what we say or post might seem inauthentic or even controlling. But after some practice, the filters become part of the best that we are. We will rarely second guess our intentions and, better still, our foot won't get caught in our mouths again.

Daniel Francis

Look Both Ways

You know the drill. Well, when you were young, someone taught you the drill. A parent or older sibling, perhaps a teacher. At some point, you were walking along a sidewalk and--about to cross the street--someone older and more experienced than you said, "Look both ways before you cross. Remember to look both ways."

Thomas Aquinas, church theologian and apologist, always studied, learned and articulated well the positions of those with whom he disagreed.

We could use a dose of Thomistic tact these days. Whenever another party is in "power"... whenever someone else is making the rules, it's so easy to look only one way.

Don't worry- I will not comment on politics or politicians. This reflection (and our website) has a higher goal of opening minds, enlarging hearts, enlightening the soul and, sometimes, nudging us all gently forward.

Nor will we knowingly try to disrespect you by offering pat answers or facile solutions. In most cases, these don't exist. If you've ever been offered one, you know they might feel good, but they miss the deeper reality and oversimplify in order to brush away.

So in the meantime, what to do? Look both ways

> 1. **Check your biases** We all have them. That's okay. But to be blinded by them is not okay. Just know that your experiences (race, culture, religion, gender, etc.) have influenced your worldview. To know what you don't know (and admit it) is not weakness but honest humility.

2. **Listen carefully** A pastor I knew used to say, "No one is smarter than all of us." Research the topic and find experts who know what they are saying. A gut feeling is helpful in some areas of life, but not when it comes to solid, scientific (or sociological) information. If 9 out of 10 dentists recommend something, it's a safe bet to listen to the majority and allow the one to be entitled to his/her opinion.

3. **Get the facts, ma'am/sir** No competent, professional journalist would ever submit a story unless and until most of the details were captured from what is called the "primary source." There are dubious news outlets which value increased viewership (and, by extension, higher ad revenue) over truth. Popularity becomes more important than principle. Fake news isn't just wrong; it's potentially lethal. The Nazi propaganda machine used fear and insecurity for morally reprehensible effects.

4. **Test the stool** Steve Magness and Brad Stulberg (of *The Growth Equation*) speak of the importance of the three legs of a stool: research, theory, and practice. If they are all there, great, go forward with your hypothesis. If two legs are there, proceed, but do so with a little extra skepticism. If you only have one of the three legs, then your idea is on shaky ground. No legs and it's almost certainly junk, or more generously, a good fiction story. Use the stool test as an evaluative tool to make sure that your thinking is clear and on the right track. If we look both ways as we enter into discussion, we can all help one another. An argument is only productive when, instead of being intent on proving "my" side, we all gain a clearer, broader picture of what is going on.

Daniel Francis

Hoop Wisdom

In mid-July, as some of you NBA fans know, the
Milwaukee Bucks ended a 50-year drought and won their
basketball championship. Alice and I watched the game
and were impressed by the young, talented Giannis
Antetokounmpo.

This ball player is equally impressive off the court, because
at the aftergame interview Antetokounmpo told a reporter:
"When you focus on the past, that's your ego... When I
focus on the future, that's my pride. I try to focus on the
present. That's humility."

The word *humility* has its origin in the word for earth,
humus, or soil. To be grounded in that earthiness is to
know your roots, to understand where you've come from.

Consider the wisdom of this tale:

> Once there was a proud preacher fresh out of the
> seminary who was full of himself. At the
> beginning of the Church service, beaming as he
> walked down the aisle, he had his face held high.
> But his sermon was a disaster- scattered, halting
> and boring. The people knew it and he felt it.
>
> As he walked out of Church, the young minister
> dropped his head in failure. That's when an old
> woman called out to him, "Preacher, had you
> walked in the way you just walked out you would
> have walked out the way you had walked in."

What are your hoop dreams? What do you focus on?
Allow yourself to be humbled by how much you and I
need to learn and grow. Prepare to be amazed today by
unforeseen discoveries. I'm not promising they will be
pleasant; I am confident they will keep you grounded.

Make Room; Create Space

The summer that my oldest brother was to turn 50, all four of us Francis men decided to celebrate his milestone birthday by hiking the Grand Canyon (we enjoyed the challenge of hiking from the north rim to the south rim in the same day- 23.9 miles in 16 hours).

The Canyon is a marvel- the rocks tell old tales of prehistoric events that carved out this... space!

And that's what it is: s-p-a-c-e... defined, for sure, by the beautiful sides and slopes and the Colorado River.

10 miles across and 277 miles long, it's a lot of SPACE.

That is precisely what beautiful buildings and parks are designed to do- provide a structure in which people can move into a space appropriate to the activity: a museum invites awe and information; a church inspires peace and devotion; a city garden prompts beauty and creativity.

On the other hand, there are those moments which hem us in and the walls might seem too close.

Perhaps the time of COVID has made it even more difficult. Some people, when experiencing anxiety, say that they find it literally hard to breathe- as if the problems and tension are squeezing them into a tight space.

It's no wonder that mental health practitioners and meditation masters alike all begin by telling their clients to breathe.

The beauty of the Grand Canyon is that it's a marvel for what it's missing. Geologists estimate that it is eroding at a rate of 1 foot every 200 years. The more rock that gets swept away the deeper it gets.

Daniel Francis

Hmmm, could there be a lesson here? Always!

Pema Chodron writes (in *When Things Fall Apart*):

> Things falling apart is a kind of testing and also a
> kind of healing. We think that the point is to pass
> the test or to overcome the problem, but the truth
> is that things don't really get solved.
> They come together and they fall apart.
> Then they come together again and fall apart
> again.
> It's just like that. The healing comes from letting
> there be room for all of this to happen: room for
> grief, for relief, for misery, for joy.
> When we think that something is going to bring
> us pleasure, we don't know what's really going to
> happen.
> When we think something is going to give us
> misery, we don't know. Letting there be room for
> not knowing is the most important thing of all.

You Doing You

I'm old enough to remember stories about popular TV personality Bishop Fulton Sheen, with his series "Life is Worth Living", attracting more prime time viewers than Milton Berle. With that invisible "angel" erasing his chalkboard, he said things like "Nothing ever happens in the world that does not happen first inside human hearts" and "We become like that which we love. If we love what is base, we become base; but if we love what is noble, we become noble."

In a similar vein, this quote by Keith Yamashita came to my attention and I admire the simplicity:

> How we spend our time is how we spend our days. How we spend our days is how our life goes. How our life goes determines whether we thought it was worth living.

To follow his logic backwards is to ask the question, How am I spending my time? What motivates me to do the things I'm doing? Am I wasting time or, worse, not paying attention to nutrition, exercise, meditation or other routines?

As a life coach, one of my initial conversations is about the REASONS for self-improvement.

Is there a sense that something is wrong and needs fixing? Fine.

But when someone feels that the something wrong is THEM, we have to do a little thought tweaking. To do what is good for you is, for sure, to solve problems (over-eating, procrastination, disorganization).

But what if there is a shift in the way you think... and you

Daniel Francis

say to yourself: "I am doing me! I'm watching what I eat
(or journaling or whatever) as an act of self-loving
kindness... not so much to fix a problem or deal with an
issue, but because it's the right, good, amazing thing to do
for myself!"

As Leo Babauta writes:

> Want to eat better?
> Focus on the joy of eating nourishing,
> whole, healthy food.

> Want to exercise?
> Focus less on losing weight and more on
> the joy of moving your body, as a loving act.

> Whatever you want to do, change the focus to
> doing something awesome for yourself:
> meditation, writing, journaling, decluttering,
> focusing on important work.

They're all loving acts, and they can feel amazing as you do
them.

Organ Recital

On his death bed, Martin Luther said, "We are all mere beggars showing other beggars where to find bread."

Isn't that the truth!

We are on this earth for a couple of decades--maybe 8 or 9-- and between birth and death it's so fulfilling to help feed others with what we have.

The best of social media is when people break digital bread with one another by showing pictures and writing posts that delight, educate and inspire. We feed each other well when what we share helps the reader a) learn something new; b) recall something known; or c) present something interesting.

For that reason, I'm going to re-post what our friend Jude recently shared on Facebook:

> My brain and heart divorced a decade ago over who was to blame about how big of a mess I have become. Eventually, they couldn't be in the same room with each other. Now my head and heart share custody of me. I stay with my brain during the week and my heart gets me on weekends. They never speak to one another. Instead, they give me the same note to pass to each other every week and their notes they send to one another always says the same thing: "This is all your fault." On Sundays, my heart complains about how my head has let me down in the past. And on Wednesday, my head lists all of the times my heart has screwed things up for me in the future. They blame each other for the state of my life there's been a lot of yelling – and crying. So lately, I've been spending a lot of time with my gut who

serves as my unofficial therapist. Most nights, I sneak out of the window in my ribcage and slide down my spine and collapse on my gut's plush leather chair that's always open for me. And I just sit sit sit sit until the sun comes up. Last evening, my gut asked me if I was having a hard time being caught between my heart and my head. I nodded. I said I didn't know if I could live with either of them anymore. "My heart is always sad about something that happened yesterday while my head is always worried about something that may happen tomorrow," I lamented. My gut squeezed my hand. "I just can't live with my mistakes of the past or my anxiety about the future," I sighed. My gut smiled and said: "In that case, you should go stay with your lungs for a while." I was confused. The look on my face gave it away. "If you are exhausted about your heart's obsession with the fixed past and your mind's focus on the uncertain future, your lungs are the perfect place for you. There is no yesterday in your lungs. There is no tomorrow there either. There is only now. There is only inhale. There is only exhale. There is only this moment. There is only breath. And in that breath, you can rest while your heart and head work their relationship out." This morning, while my brain was busy reading tea leaves and while my heart was staring at old photographs, I packed a little bag and walked to the door of my lungs. Before I could even knock, she opened the door with a smile and as a gust of air embraced me she said: "What took you so long?"

- by John Roedel

Spare Some Change?

"Home, sweet home!"

As much as we enjoyed a recent mini-vacation for a wedding and family visit, it was so good to turn into our driveway, tread barefoot on our wonderfully worn carpet and sleep in our own bed. As people who are trying to be more mindful and not react, traveling is replete with opportunities to grow in patience, perspective and understanding.

Geoffrey Chaucer wrote that "familiarity breeds contempt", but I find that change is just as effective at times. The upside is that unless change happens, we risk becoming stagnant, staid and stale.

Here are some tips for navigating the inevitable vicissitudes of life: Each opportunity is a classroom.

When plans suddenly shift, it's easy to get frustrated. What if, instead, we embraced change to get better at being flexible, nimble and resilient?

Change invites us to slow down and be present. Think about it- when confronted with an obstacle, impasse or predicament caused by change, you can bewail or breath.

Annoyance occurs when what is happening is not what we expect and so we are left "out of control." What if we focused instead on what is right here, what we can control (for instance, our breathing, which then slows down our heart rate)?

My mother died just before Mass began on the last Sunday in April of 2001. Dressed so beautifully for the First Communion of my twin nieces, in 15 minutes, after collapsing from heart failure, she was "gone."

So, when the next moment can be dramatically different at any time, the response is not to distrust life but rather embrace all that happens. It's difficult. But what's the option?

If, rather than fighting uncertainty, we simply notice it as neither friend nor foe, then we get familiar with an unfamiliar terrain called the next moment.

Practice leaning into what happens, no matter what happens. Learning to open to what is unfolding, unplanned and unpredictable is practice ... at times the toughest work we do. We don't practice to become perfect; we practice to be unflappable, grounded and nonreactive. Structure is helpful, but don't get attached.

I began this reflection by telling you how nice it is to return home after vacation. In our house, we have wonderful rituals surrounding morning meditation, coffee and tea breaks, meals, our evening walk, etc. Structure helps to create some order to get things done: email, messages, finances, chores, planning, exercise ... but (there's always a "but") clinging to structure can produce frustration when the unexpected happens.

What to do then? This is when mindfulness (helped by meditation) comes in and allows us to see change as part of life, not an obstacle.

With lots of practice, you too can say, "Change, sweet change!"

Too Much Positivity?

Is there such a thing as too much positivity? Quick answer: no, unless...

As you know from our name, Alive 'n Well, we believe in helping create a world that works for everybody; a society that is civil, even if there are important heated discussions; a country that upholds the rights of everyone regardless of how "different" they might be from us.

In other words, we embrace a positive way of regarding whatever is happening now.

We also are aware that positivity might seem scant for those affected by the pandemic, climate change or suffering of any kind. We know that--as a matter of science--the refusal to see life's difficulties and denying uncomfortable experiences can sicken someone emotionally or worse.

"Toxic positivity" is ultimately a denial of reality. Rather than saying "stay positive" to someone in a real crisis, listening to them without judgment or unsolicited advice conveys one's own positivity AS sympathy... wordlessly.

As the gratitude researcher Robert Emmons of UC Davis writes, "To deny that life has its share of disappointments, frustrations, losses, hurts, setbacks, and sadness would be unrealistic and untenable. Life is suffering. No amount of positive thinking exercises will change this truth."

So, what's helpful?

Psychologist and Holocaust survivor Viktor Frankl coined the phrase "tragic optimism." This way of living inspires a search for meaning amid the inevitable tragedies of human existence. Sometimes nothing short of miraculous are the ways people have been *re-born* after going through tragedy, grief and loss: they have greater appreciation of life and intense love of others, increased compassion, sense of purpose and even spiritual renewal.

Frankl wrote, "No matter what happens, we always possess the ability to decide what to make of our condition."

Optimizing a tragedy changes how you process the event and it upgrades your worldview.

Kristi Nelson, the executive director of A Network for Grateful Living, faced her own mortality at the age of 33, when she received a cancer diagnosis and had to undergo multiple surgeries, chemo and radiation. Nevertheless, she writes that she was constantly on the lookout for opportunities to cultivate gratefulness:

> I was in the hospital, separated from all my friends and family and tethered to all kinds of IVs and dealing with pain. And yet, I had nurses and technicians and doctors and cleaners who came into my room every single day. I remember thinking, what if this is my whole world now, what if this is all I have? And then I thought, I can always love these people.

You can stay negative all you want, preferring to blame, complain, dismiss or demean. But I know few people who are happy "there." They say that misery loves company. I say that it DEMANDS it!

Rather, find a way to be grateful for at least one thing each day and you will never have a case of toxic positivity.

Death Be Not Feared

We heard on the news yesterday that Colin Powell died. It feels like he's been around ever since I was conversing about politics.

Powell's death hit me similar to when I'm watching one of those Awards shows and they have the section called "In Memoriam."

As they list the names of those who died in the past year, there are always a few that make me think, "Oh not... not [so and so]. When?"

Poet, essayist, and philosopher Audre Lorde writes:

> In becoming forcibly and essentially aware of my mortality, and of what I wished and wanted for my life, however short it might be, priorities and omissions became strongly etched in a merciless light, and what I most regretted were my silences. Of what had I ever been afraid?

Lorde was dying from cancer when she wrote these words. That last line stops my breath: "Of what had I ever been afraid?" There are strains of beautiful Psalm 23 in this.

It makes me wonder if sometimes I let my fears and desires control me rather than living from my place of peace and joy.

> Tell a wise person or else keep silent
> for those who do not understand
> will mock it right away.
> I praise what is truly alive
> what longs to be burned to death....
> ...And so long as you have not experienced

229

Daniel Francis

> this: to die and so to grow
> you are only a troubled guest
> on the dark earth.
>
> — Johann Wolfgang Von
> Goethe

When Other People Become Teachers

Robert Frost once quipped: "Home is the place where, when you have to go there, they have to take you in."

My eldest sister was diagnosed with early-onset Alzheimer's nearly two years ago and it has brought us seven siblings closer together.

Via Zoom or conference calls, emails and a special text thread, we try and help each other help Darlene as best we can.

But the diagnosis has also created its own challenges and lessons. For example, how much independence do you allow without the risk of an accident? Who monitors the medications and which sibling takes time off for the doctor visits?

In this and in other situations, I've learned that we are all so different- family members, closest friends, soul partners....

No matter how well-meaning good intentions may be, there are always frustration points. We respond so differently to a variety of circumstances.

Rather than drive us crazy, maybe the lesson is to manage only what is ours to manage.

Trying to change others, wanting our kids to behave this way, our neighbors not to act that way... our colleagues, friends, the government ... it's an endless battle of wills. Unless...

Unless you realize that you can control only what you can control.

You see, other people can become *teachers*. Let me share

Daniel Francis

what I've learned:

- Some people do seek advice (that's why I'm a Life Coach); most people, however, just want to be listened to
- People can live their lives however they want, with or without my permission
- If I don't see the good in someone I am probably blinded by my own ego insisting that "my way is better"
- When someone--especially a loved one-- is being exasperating, to remind myself that they are probably not coping well with something... and to empathize with this
- Truly, to know how much I appreciate when others afford me this empathy when **I'm** difficult to deal with

I'm still far from perfect at this and sometimes I'm not even good at this, but when I find my peace point (as my wife and I like to call it), it helps. Then dealing with other people is less frustrating and the process helps me to be more mindful while also enhancing my relationships.

At Alive 'n Well, this--and so much more--is what we wish for all of you.

Create Space

You know what a knee-jerk reaction is.

In the clinic, the doctor taps your patella with a hammer and your brain bypasses neurons producing impulses in the hamstrings that involuntarily raise your leg.

Likewise, there are social "hammers" which get reactions out of us.

Also called "button pushers", these external stimuli can get us worked up.

The good news is that we are equipped with the ability to pause before we react.

Philosophers say that this pause is where our freedom resides.

A quick review: to **react** is to be impulsive and unthinking; to **respond** is to be conscious and intentional.

One way to respond rather than react is to name what you are feeling.

When something happens that is hard for you to handle, try to say what is happening: for instance, *I feel tightness in my chest, I feel anxiety in my throat* or *I feel anger in my heart.*

Does it take away the feeling?

Perhaps not right away, but it will eventually lead you to a place of peace which will become more familiar to you- and a better place than being on edge, feeling tightness, anxiety or anger.

In moments of utter craziness, intense darkness or just

233

wordless absurdity, let your inner friend say to you, "You won't always feel the way you are feeling right now." Take comfort from this and trust this friend.

It's one of the best parts of you.

Freedom and Joy

My brother Jim used to travel by plane for his work a lot more than he does now. And for a while, so did I.

In an amazing coincidence, once he called me while we were both inside the Twin Cities airport in Minnesota- he departing as I was arriving. No time to meet, but we laughed at the irony -closer than a mile and yet connected only by cell phone.

A couple of weeks ago my niece gave us a concert via Zoom. Probably 1400 miles away and yet wonderfully connected by smiles and strums and sounds.

Two people can live in the same house or sit in the same pew in Church and the distance can be greater than the coldness of a mechanical kiss or perfunctory sign of peace.

We recently watched a documentary of a woman who was raised in the Arctic, went back again in her 20s and then returned in her 50s. She told lessons of survival, simplicity, gratitude and strength.

And then I read an article in the *New York Times* about a 37-year-old woman diagnosed with Stage IV colon cancer rejecting the idea of a bucket list. She just wanted to enjoy living and loving and experiencing life as she could.

What do airports have to do with the Arctic and technology with terminal illness?

It's about being awake, aware, alive and in touch with what is going on now- certainly outside of me (what I can change) but most acutely that truth that is deep within.

Nothing is as close to us as the true self that persistently and wonderfully bugs us to live in freedom and joy.

Daniel Francis

Keep Learning

It is said that the one who only has him or herself as a
teacher has a fool for a student.

Similarly, research shows that most people who attended
the best schools continue to study and seek out mentors.

If you learn from TV and talk shows, good for you. If,
however, these media only serve as an echo chamber, be
careful.

I loved vacationing with my friend, Bob. He would stop to
read every plaque, post, sign and memorial on a tour or in
a museum. While his wife poked fun at him, his hunger for
knowledge was inspiring.

In the past couple of years, I've had the privilege of
helping two men write their memoirs.

What amazed me is their ability to view nearly every
significant event in their public, professional or private
sphere as having been a *constitutive part of their life's curriculum.*
It's no coincidence that both are voracious readers.

I've learned a lot from these gentlemen.

There are so many wise women and men "out there"...
who have gone through experiences you have--good as
well as difficult--and learned from them; others have
encountered situations you'll likely encounter one day.

Let these be your gurus. Listen to them. Cultivate the
wisdom that will help not only you but the people who
learn from you.

Class Is (always) In Session

One thing I love asking friends old and new is: What are you reading right now that is stirring you up?

How about you? Besides this little book, what is making you think higher and better, fuller and wider so that you're always learning allowing you to embrace the wonder and joy that class is always in session!

Daniel Francis

ABOUT THE AUTHOR

Daniel Francis, co-founder of Alive 'n Well, LLC, is a life coach. Born the sixth of seven children, he grew up a traveler-on three continents before his 6th birthday with a father in the Navy and a mother who loved globetrotting. In 2014, he began DMF Coaching which contracts support to individuals for one-on-one life coaching and offers speaking opportunities to groups. A former Catholic priest, Daniel has been a motivational speaker for the past 26 years and has given presentations in over 250 cities in 12 countries and on 4 continents. He and his wife live in Tampa and enjoy gardening, meditation, reading, exercise and (in non-pandemic times) trying out new local establishments.

For more information and for daily and weekly inspiration, go to www.alivenwell.net.

Made in the USA
Middletown, DE
04 November 2021

51654122R10135